Francis Turner Palgrave, John Campbell Shairp

Glen Desseray and other Poems - Lyrical and Elegiac

Francis Turner Palgrave, John Campbell Shairp

Glen Desseray and other Poems - Lyrical and Elegiac

ISBN/EAN: 9783744712323

Printed in Europe, USA, Canada, Australia, Japan

Cover: Foto ©Thomas Meinert / pixelio.de

More available books at **www.hansebooks.com**

GLEN DESSERAY
AND OTHER POEMS
By J. C. SHAIRP

O FOR truth-breathèd music ! soul-like lays !
Not of vain-glory born, nor love of praise,
But welling purely from profound heart-springs,
That lie deep down amid the life of things,
And singing on, heedless though mortal ear
Should never their lone murmur overhear !

GLEN DESSERAY

AND OTHER POEMS

LYRICAL AND ELEGIAC

BY

JOHN CAMPBELL SHAIRP

LL.D., LATE PRINCIPAL OF THE UNITED COLLEGE, ST. ANDREWS, AND
PROFESSOR OF POETRY IN THE UNIVERSITY OF OXFORD

EDITED BY

FRANCIS T. PALGRAVE

LL.D. EDINBURGH

London

MACMILLAN AND CO.

AND NEW YORK

1888

TO THE AUTHOR'S EARLY FRIENDS
WHO HAVE SURVIVED HIM;
TO THE FRIENDS OF LATER YEARS;
AND TO ALL WHO MISS HIS PRESENCE,
AND WHO VALUE HIS THOUGHTS, IN PROSE AND VERSE;

THESE POEMS

ARE, FOR HIS SAKE, DEDICATED BY

E. S.

PREFACE

IN carrying out the labour of love entrusted to me by those most nearly connected with this much-honoured and regretted Friend, my wish has been to present such a selection from his published and manuscript verse as shall do justice to one of the most sincere and high-minded poets of our century. Nothing, as the verdict of Time constantly but vainly proves, is more insecure than contemporary judgments upon contemporary work in art and literature. Indeed, "Fame herself," as a great critic observes, even when she seems firmly established, "has but a short memory." I shall therefore attempt no forecasting or estimate of what Shairp's place in our poetry may prove, beyond this, which can be safely hazarded;—that in the following poems no sensitive mind can fail to find the note of what his friend Matthew Arnold has excellently described as *distinction;*—the note of a pure, refined, modest originality. It is beyond question a voice, not an echo, which we hear. Even in his ballad-songs, easily as that form invites to imitation, Shairp preserves an individual quality;

nor, devoted as he was to Wordsworth, do we trace in the lyrics more than a few slight reminiscences of his manner.

In a Garland like this, chosen, unhappily, from the silent treasury of the dead, where but little certainty can be felt which pieces might have seemed to the writer worthy preservation, my endeavour in selecting has been to follow the only safe rule—admit such poems alone as fairly seem on a level with the poet's best work. A choice thus made is difficult, and can hardly hope to satisfy every one. If, therefore, any readers—Scottish readers in particular—find omissions to regret, let me ask their pardon on the plea that I have tried to do what is most loyal to Shairp's memory, and would far rather bear the blame of bad taste on my own account, than follow those deplorable examples of exhaustive publication by which a mistaken " Love of Letters " has too often

> Swampt the sacred poets with themselves,—

sweeping-in the rejected fragments of the artist's studio, and irreverently alloying with inferior ore the pure gold of genius.

Although some short lyrics from the volume published by Shairp in 1864 (under the title of the narrative poem, *Kilmahoe*, which fills the larger portion of it) have been included, yet the present book contains in general the writer's maturer work, selected either from the papers in the hands of his family, or from pieces which have hitherto had only a magazine publication. These latter I have regarded as bearing, on the whole, the seal of Shairp's approval. But his own corrected copies, where possible, are here followed; whilst, in case of the manuscripts, which have not always received the last touches of the writer, I have ventured to omit a very few lines.

For the notes, glossarial and illustrative, I am mainly indebted to the Rev. T. Sinton, Minister of Glengarry, and to Mr. Bayne of Helensburgh. My wish, at first, was to ask Mr. Sinton for a transliteration into English sounds of the many Gaelic place-names which occur. But a few specimens proved that this would be well-nigh practically impossible in the case of languages differing so deeply in their intonation. And it may be feared that the ignorant indifference, descending sometimes into stupid hostility, with which the beautiful Celtic dialects yet surviving in our islands are regarded by almost all except those to whom they are mother-tongues, would have rendered translation of the sound and the significance of these relics of the past an almost useless and unvalued labour.

It is also probable that some readers—in Scotland especially—may find the foot-notes over numerous.

Here I would plead that Poetry, in this age of facile prose, requires every assistance to attract and hold its audience. Better that fifty should find an explanation superfluous, than one find a difficulty unsolved.

As the narrative of Principal Shairp's life is in other and more competent hands, it remains for me now only to offer some brief words on the aim and character of these poems, on their sentiment and style. Such critical notes, it is almost a truism to say, can never really be adequate. As it is with the special perfume of rose or lily, so the quality by which the melody of Mozart differs from that of Beethoven, the charm with which the childless Reynolds rendered the children of his canvas;—Vergilian magic, even when interpreted by the master-hand of Cardinal Newman;—Shakespearean felicity;—of all these things the essence is indefinable, the secret inscrutable. Through much of the Palace of Art our guides may lead us; but to the "inmost enchanted fountain"—the mystery of the Maker—we never penetrate. And stars of a lesser magnitude, if only they be stars, shining with light of their own, each has also a quality peculiar to itself, an influence not rained from any other. This premised, let me take some of the following poems, and try if I can put into words some slight shadow of this influence, of this essence, so that those readers may enter into them with greater facility, to whom Shairp has been hitherto unknown. And although a poet in the end is his own best interpreter, yet in this case there is the further reason for a short introduction, that the ways and thoughts of the Highland peasantry, remote and alien from most of us,—so far as the remorseless wheels of the car of civilization have yet spared them, —were my Friend's special care, and form everywhere the moral atmosphere with which the wild landscape of his native land is suffused and invested.

Glen Desseray is a little Epic, an Epyllion, as the ancients said, of the Highlands. Into this poem, his most sustained attempt, Shairp has thrown his deepest feeling on the western mountain regions,—"the Visions of the hills, And Souls of lonely places":—throughout connecting the landscape, as it unfolds itself, with the human interests of the story. The narrative covers some sixty or seventy years from the middle of the eighteenth century, setting before us, as its principal theme, the romantic wanderings of Prince Charles Edward, whilst passing through that cloud of danger and defeat, when the noble and gallant elements of his character shone forth most brilliantly;—contrasted with the scene of a Chief's return from exile; followed by a second gathering of clansmen for foreign service, and, finally, by a glance at that "clearing of the glens" which, during the last hundred years, has so changed even the very landscape of the Highlands:—whilst incidental pictures of Gaelic life, manners, and character add animation to the long and varied tapestry which the poet has embroidered for us. Since Walter Scott, who practically revealed, whilst he in some sense created, the Highlands for his countrymen, has any one—any poet, at least—put them before us with such vividness, such charm, such inner truth, as Shairp?

Skill in devising plot has not at any time been common among our poets; their genius turns much more to sentiment, character, or description; and it is in these elements that the strength of *Glen Desseray* will be found. The narrative wanders discursively down the stream of Time, whilst tracing the incidents of the tale through the long glens of North-Western Scotland. It has something of the labyrinthine aspect of wild Nature, of her apparent aimlessness. But throughout is felt one intense fervour of interest in the land of the Gael and its romantic natives; one pure and lofty passion of patriotism. It has the unity of sentiment, the unity of heart.

It may be noticed, as a fine stroke of art, that in Shairp's first version of this poem a love-episode was given in Cantos V and VI, but rejected in favour of the more pathetic and unusual picture of Muriel's sisterly devotion and the noble fervour of friendship between Angus and Ronald; which we may liken to the similar groups of Chaucer's Palamon and Arcite, the Amis and Amil of the beautiful ancient French legend, or the love between David and Jonathan, of which the poet himself reminds us.

Description of nature forms a large portion of Shairp's work. His landscape is indicated by brief characteristic features, calling up in succession clear images before the mind; but there is little realistic detail, no attempt at "word-painting" for its own sake. And at every instant the scene is connected with human life or human feeling. It thus suggests a picture, yet could not be reproduced on canvas. Shairp, in a word, has followed that eternal aesthetic canon of *appropriateness*, which demands that each of the Fine Arts shall render its subject solely through the method peculiar to itself.

If we turn from the manner to the matter of Shairp's landscape, in two marked features it seems to differ from that of Wordsworth, asserting in these its own originality, or, as we might also say, its adherence to the actual facts. The narrow area of the English Lake district contrasts with the wild Highland regions by a finished beauty, a soft richness of effect, an amenity, to put it in one significant word, which can hardly be found elsewhere, I think, nearer than the mountain lakes,—*te, Lari maxume*,—and those others, which are the charm of North-West Italy. It was the wildness, the vast *loca pastorum deserta*, the asperity of desolation, the glory touched with gloom of the Highland world, by which Shairp was penetrated. This aspect of the soul of Nature he has characterized in his fine essay on Keble, when speaking of "her infinite and unhuman side, which yields no symbols to soothe man's yearnings." Nowhere, he writes, is this "so borne in on man as in the midst of the vast deserts of the earth, or in the presence of the mountains, which seem so impassive and unchangeable. Their strength and permanence so contrast with man—of few years and full of trouble; they are so indifferent to his feelings or his destiny. He may smile or weep, he may live or die; they care not. They are the same in all their ongoings, happen what will to him. They respond to the sunrises and the sunsets, but not to his sympathies. All the same they fulfil their mighty functions, careless though no human eye should ever look on them."

How different is this tone from that habitual with Wordsworth! To him, the sympathy between the outer world and the inner world of man, the echo and the lessons with which the landscape almost consciously responds to the human heart, the penetration of all Nature by the

Being that is in the clouds and air,

are the central ideas and convictions of his soul. But the note struck in the words above quoted from Shairp is dominant in his own landscape-work, and it corresponds with the human sentiment which, — as must always be found in true landscape, whether painted in words or in colours, — atmospheres every picture. The disappearance of the old Highland life; of the clans, not indeed as they were in the lawless years of old, but in their later pastoral phase; the clearing of the glens under a long train of circumstances which I can only note without discussion, — all these features of human activity and joy and desolation seem to supply a soul to his delineation of scenery, in harmony with its innermost character. What the memory of the lost friend was to Tennyson in his great lyrical elegy, the warmth of tender sympathy, of chastened enthusiasm for the Gael, is in the poems before us. We have here the second point of difference from Wordsworth. For that great poet, we know, more or less saw his own heart, his own thoughts and emotions, mirrored for him in Nature; not, indeed, in that mood of a somewhat morbid sadness which, also, has lent a charm and interest of its own to some splendid poetry of the latter days, — a Childe Harold or an Alastor, — but with a sanity and breadth of view which lifts his landscape above mere "subjective" imaginings. Wordsworth, speaking for and from himself, speaks most often for humanity in general; he has, we might perhaps say, an impersonal personality. He learned much, doubtless, from his simple-hearted neighbours: but they are rarely part of his landscape. *Vox hominem sonat;* "Men, as they are men within themselves," so far as his experience went,—not the men of Westmoreland, were Wordsworth's real theme.

There are passages, of course, in which Shairp's own feeling for nature, his own deep and large-hearted religious faith, reveal themselves. Such is the striking reflection in *Glen Desseray* (C. iii, 5), where he touches on the blankness felt, when, in some scene to which we have eagerly come, filled with the remembrance of a glorious Past, we find no trace of human sentiment or human deed surviving; in the *Return to Nature;* or the profoundly-imagined *Wilderness.* So, again, in those poems where a peculiar tenderness of personal sympathy gives its tone to the landscape; as in the *Three Friends in Yarrow,* the *Spring, 1876,* and the lovely *Bush aboon Traquair,*—distinguished above all Shairp's early lyrics by such gracious exquisiteness of sentiment and melody, that it should singly be enough to ensure him an abiding place in that unique and delightful company,—the songwriters of Scotland. Yet, in his poems of this class, self is never the leading note; and, on a survey of his whole work, it must be felt that, within the measure of his faculty, Shairp ranks in the great army, —the greater army (I should venture to call it),—of "objective" poets.

To this sphere, at any rate, conclusively belong many of the latter pieces in this volume. The very few brief songs it presents, which, if not strictly ballads, have sprung from the ballad, and are its fine flower in a more condensed and lyrical form,—the *Cailleach*, the *Devorguilla* (despite its trochaic metre, with the peculiar difficulties of which Shairp, like Wordsworth before him, seems to me to contend in vain), the graceful *Hairst Rig*,—all "found" (to follow a convenient Scottish usage) on reality ; all have an underground, not of mere sentiment, the common defect in such songs, but of true individuality. But as the most noteworthy specimen of Shairp's power in this field we may rank the dialogue *Lost on Schihallion*. This has a tragic pathos, a holy simplicity and grandeur as of Nature herself, which make it a fit companion picture to Lady Anne Lindsay's well-known masterpiece.

The power shown in these little lyrics,—and, under a different guise, in the ode on the Battle of the Alma,—may make us regret that Shairp did not write more upon such directly "objective" subjects. In them he has not that flash and movement of life wherein Scott is well-nigh alone amongst our nineteenth century poets. Yet these ballad-verses (to which the Dyeing and Weaving of the Plaid, in the Fifth Canto of *Glen Desseray*, may be added), display a measure of Scott's Homeric simplicity and downright current of narration; a truly Greek abstinence from decoration for decoration's sake. The poet's eye is on his object, and his object alone; the verse has the peculiar charm of *disinterestedness;* a quality which, I think, can only be imparted to his work by a soul completely freed and purified from egotism.

It is the presence of such a soul,—to touch here a deeper note,—that we feel in those strains of higher mood which close the book; although, as with poetry of this order is inevitable, the voice comes from the inner world of personal thought and the heart's deepest feelings. In these poems Shairp, I think, had often before his mind the words or writings of our highly loved and admired Arthur Clough. Shairp, indeed, enjoyed a healthy happiness of faith, which, in the beautiful verse left us by Clough,—"too cruelly distraught," and dying too soon,—may be less perceptible; but they both

pii Vates et Phoebo digna locuti,

upon every line of their "soul-songs" have set the same stamp of an absolute sincerity.

These large-hearted poems, however, are best left to speak for themselves. Clough's name carries us to that remaining section of Shairp's work, in which, again, he may claim a field of his own, little laboured by recent English writers. The large simplicity of his style, his strongly-marked "objective" habit of mind, are nowhere better seen than in the *Character Pieces*, as I have ventured to entitle them. Many readers in England will recognize the skill of portraiture in the *Balliol Scholars;* to the faithfulness of which, having myself been privileged not long after to enter the same gifted company, I can bear witness. It is, truly, a group drawn with the gracious insight of a judgment evenly poised between discernment and sympathy;—the love of truthfulness, and the truthfulness that only comes of love.

Those, doubtless, who knew the *Highland Students* whom Shairp taught and commemorated, would find in his three monumental elegies the same sympathetic fidelity. None of his work seems to me more original, more entirely his own, than this little series; and in the management of that most difficult of all our metres—the blank verse—it is eminently successful. Wordsworth's magnificent *Michael* must, indeed, have been in his mind when he framed these clear-cut and tender memorials; but the disciple was worthy of the master.

Returning now for a moment to the leading poem:— It will, I think, be felt that *Glen Desseray* is eminently characteristic both of Shairp's own "aspects of poetry," and of his own work as a poet. In the beautiful volume of Lectures given from the Chair in which, *non passibus aequis*, it has been my sad honour to follow the Friend too early summoned to the Life Unseen, he has defined the qualities which, to his mind, were central in Poetry :—

"One of the first characteristics of the genuine and healthy poetic nature is this—it is rooted rather in the heart than in the head. Human-heartedness is the soil from which all its other gifts originally grow, and are continually fed. The true poet is not an eccentric creature, not a mere artist living only for art, not a dreamer or a dilettante, sipping the nectar of existence while he keeps aloof from its deeper interests. He is, above all things, a man among his fellow-men, with a heart that beats in sympathy with theirs, only larger, more open, more sensitive, more intense." And again: "Whenever the soul comes vividly in contact with any fact, truth, or existence, whenever it realises and takes them home to itself with more than common intensity, out of that meeting of the soul and its object there arises a thrill of joy, a glow of emotion; and the expression of that *glow*, that *thrill*, is poetry."

In a similar train of thought, putting always the natural expression of the heart as his first and last

requirement, Shairp elsewhere draws a decided line,
—a line which I venture to think too decided,—between what he speaks of as the "pure" and the
"ornate" styles in Poetry,—epithets which, indeed, in
accordance with the passages just quoted, reveal the
style that he loved and practised, but by which the
knot of the question is rather cut than loosened.
Hence it may, I think, be said of Shairp that his bias
rendered him in some degree unwilling or unable to
recognize, with all its due force, that Poetry, in
Florizel's phrase,

> Is an art
> Which does mend Nature,—change it rather; but
> The art itself is nature.

It was doubtless due in some degree to this deep-seated mode of regarding poetry that in Shairp's
work we may at times find an apparent carelessness
in the choice of words, a want of finish in style,
an absence of that evenness in metrical flow which
the ear demands. Truly might he have said of
himself, with Dante, while still on the Mount of
Probation—

> Io mi son un che, quando
> Amore spira, noto, ed a quel modo
> Ch' ei detta dentro, vo significando.

These little lapses,—these proofs of natural freshness

and freedom, we might also better say,—are perhaps seen most in his earlier verse; in regard to the later, we must recollect that the chords of the harp were broken, before the minstrel could complete his melody.

  Qui mai più no ; ma rivedrenne altrove.

F. T. P.

Jan. 9, 1888

CONTENTS

LYRICS OF HIGHLAND LIFE AND LANDSCAPE

GLEN DESSERAY; OR, THE SEQUEL OF CULLODEN—
                                                                               PAGE
    Canto First—The Chief Restored . . . 3
    Canto Second—Bothain-Airidh; or, The Shealings 22
    Canto Third—On the Track of the Prince . . 36
    Canto Fourth—The Home by Lochourn . . 45
    Canto Fifth—The War Summons . . . 53
    Canto Sixth—The Soldier's Return . . . 68

THE MOUNTAIN WALK 88

A DREAM OF GLEN-SALLACH 98

THE MOOR OF RANNOCH 100

THE LASS OF LOCH LINNE 104

THE FOREST OF SLI'-GAOIL 106

RETURN TO NATURE 108

CAILLEACH BEIN-Y-VREICH 110

DESOLATION 112

A CRY FROM CRAIG-ELLACHIE 114

BEN CRUACHAN 119

	PAGE
ON VISITING DRUIM-A LIATH	124
SCHIHALLION	128
TORRIDON GLEN	130
LOCH TORRIDON	134
PROGNOSTIC	139
THE WILDERNESS	140
THE HIGHLAND RIVER	144
LOST ON SCHIHALLION	146
WILD FLOWERS IN JUNE	149
ALT CUCHIN DOUN	157
THE SHEPHERD'S HOUSE	159
AUTUMN IN THE HIGHLANDS—	
October	162
Garth Castle	164
CLATTO	167
AUCHMORE	170
DRUMUACHDAR	172

LOWLAND LYRICS

THE BUSH ABOON TRAQUAIR	179
THRIEVE CASTLE	182
DEVORGUILLA; OR THE ABBEY OF THE SWEET HEART	185
THEN AND NOW	188

CONTENTS

	PAGE
THE BLUE BELLS	191
THE HAIRST RIG	193
MANOR WATER	195
SONG OF THE SOUTH COUNTREE	198
THREE FRIENDS IN YARROW	201

CHARACTER PIECES

BALLIOL SCHOLARS, 1840-1843	209
DEAN STANLEY AT ST. ANDREWS	221
THE DEATH OF PRINCE ALBERT	223
ON THE DEATH OF SIR JAMES SIMPSON	225
SPRING, 1876	228
HIGHLAND STUDENTS—	
I	231
II	236
III	242

VARIA

THE BATTLE OF THE ALMA	249
GRASMERE	253
PARTING	254
POETIC TRUTH	256
PRAYER	257
RELIEF	258

	PAGE
MEMORIES	259
HIDDEN LIFE	262
"I HAVE A LIFE"	264
"'TWIXT GLEAMS OF JOY" . . .	265
ILLUSTRATIVE NOTES	269
INDEX OF FIRST LINES . . .	277

LYRICS OF HIGHLAND LIFE
AND LANDSCAPE

GLEN DESSERAY;

OR

THE SEQUEL OF CULLODEN [1]

CANTO FIRST

THE CHIEF RESTORED

I

Eighty years have come and gone
Since on the dark December night,
East and west Glen Desseray shone
With fires illumining holm and height—
A sudden and a marvellous sight!
Never since dread Culloden days
The Bens [2] had seen such beacons blaze;
But those were lurid, boding bale
And vengeance on the prostrate Gael,
These on the tranquil night benign,

---

[1] For the scheme and idea of this Poem, see Note at end.
[2] *Bens*, used of the loftier mountains.

As with a festal gladness, shine.
One from the knoll that shuts the glen
Flings down the loch a beard of fire;
Up on the braesides,[1] homes of men
Answer each other, high and higher,
Across the valley with a voice
Of light that shouts, Rejoice, Rejoice.
Nor less, within, the red torch-pine
And peat-fires piled on hearth combine
To brighten rafters glossy-clear
With lustre strange for many a year.
And blithe sounds since the Forty-five
Unheard within these homes revive,
Now with the pibroch, now with song,
Driving the night in joy along.
What means it all? how can it be
Such sights and sounds of revelry
From a secluded silent race
Break on the solitary place?
That music sounds, these beacons burn
—In honour of a Chief's return.

II

Long had our people sat in gloom
Within their own Glen Desseray,
O'er-shadowed by the cloud of doom

[1] *Braesides*, hillsides.

That gathered on that doleful day,
When ruin from Culloden moor
The hills of Albyn darkened o'er,
From east to west, from shore to shore.
No loyal home in glen or strath
But felt the red-coats' vengeful wrath;
Yet most on these our glens it fell,
They that had served the Prince so well;
Who first the friendless Prince had hailed,
When his foot touched the Moidart strand,
And last had sheltered, ere he sailed
Forever from his Father's land.

III

No home in all this glen but mourned
Some loved one laid in battle low;
Who from the headlong rout returned
   Reserved for heavier woe,
From their own hills with helpless gaze
Beheld their flocks by spoilers driven,
Their roofs with ruthless fires ablaze,
   Reddening the dark night heaven.
Some on the mountains hunted down
With their blood stained the heather brown,
And many more were driven forth
Lorn exiles from their native earth;
While he, the gentle and the brave

Lochiel, who led them, doomed to bide
A life-long exile, found a grave
Far from his own Loch Arkaig side.
And when at last war guns were hushed,
And back to wasted farms they fared,
With bitter memories, spirits crushed,
The few, whom sword and famine spared,
Saw the old order banished, saw
The old clan-ties asunder torn,
For their chief's care a factor's scorn,
And iron rule of Saxon law.
One rent to him constrained to bring,
"The German lairdie," called a king;
They o'er the sea in secret sent
To their own Chief another rent
In his far place of banishment.

IV

When forty years had come and gone,
At length on lone Glen Desseray shone
A day like sudden spring new-born
From the womb of winter dark and lorn,
The day for which all hearts had yearned,
With tidings of their Chief returned.
Yea, spring-like on that wintry time,
The tidings came from southron clime,
That he their leal long-exiled lord

Ere long would meet their hearts' desires,
Their chieftain to his own restored
Another home would re-instate,
Would build the house long desolate—
The ruined home where dwelt his sires:
Not he who led the fatal war,
No! nor his son—they sleep afar,
But sprung from the old heroic tree
An offshoot in the third degree.

V

It wakened mountain, loch, and glen,
That cry—" Lochiel comes back again;"
Loch Leven and Loch Linnhe's shore
Shout to the head of Nevis Ben,
The crags and corries [1] of Màmore
Rang to that word, " He comes again."
High up along Lochaber Braes
Fleeter than fiery cross it sped,
The Great Glen heard with glad amaze
And rolled it on to Loch Askaig-head.
From loch to hill the tidings spread,
And smote with joy each dwelling place
Of Camerons—clachan,[2] farm, and shiel,[3]
And the long glens that interlace

---

[1] *Corries*, deep circular hollows in the hills.
[2] *Clachan*, village. [3] *Shiel*, shepherd's hut, chalet.

The mountains piled benorth Lochiel.
Glen-Mallie and Glen-Camgarie
Resounded to the joyful cry,
Westward with the sunset fleeing,
It roused the homes of green Glenpean ;
Glen Kinzie tossed it on—unbarred
It swept o'er rugged Màm-Clach-Ard,
Start at these sounds the rugged bounds
Of Arisaig, Moidart, Morar, and Knoydart,
Down to the ocean's misty bourn
By dark Loch Nevish and Lochourn.

VI

Many a heart that news made glad,
Hearts that for years scant gladness had,
But him it gladdened more than all,
The Patriarch of Glen Desseray,
Dwelling where sunny Sheneval
From the green braeside fronts noon-day,
My grandsire, Ewen Cameron, then
Numbering three score years and ten.
Of all our clansmen still alive,
None in the gallant Forty-five
Had borne a larger, nobler part,
 Had seen or suffered more ;
Thenceforward on no living heart
  Was graven richer store

Of mournful memories and sublime,
Gleaned from that wild adventurous time.

VII

For when the Prince's summons called,
    Answered to that brave appeal
No nobler heart than Archibald,
    Brother worthy of Lochiel,
Him following fain, my grandsire flew
To the gathering by Loch Shiel,
Thence a foster-brother true
Followed him through woe and weal.
Nothing could these two divide,
Marching forward side by side,
Two friends, each of the other sure,—
Through Prestonpans and Falkirk Muir.
But when on dark Culloden day
A wounded man Gillespic lay,
My grandsire bore him to the shore
And helped him over seas away.
Seven years went by; less fiercely burned
The conqueror's vengeance 'gainst the Gael—
Gillespic Cameron fain returned
    To see his native vale.
Waylaid and captured on his road
    By the basest souls alive,
His blood upon the scaffold flowed,

Last victim of the Forty-five.
Thenceforth wrapt in speechless gloom
   Ewen mourned that lovely head;
His heart become a living tomb
   Haunted by memory of the dead.
Never more from his lips fell
Name of him he loved so well,
But the less he spake, the more his heart
'Mid these sad memories dwelt apart.

VIII

But when on lone Glen Desseray broke
The first flash of that joyous cry,
From his long dream old Ewen woke—
   I wot his heart leapt high.
No news like that had fallen on him,
Within his cabin smoky dim
For forty summers long and more.
Straightway beyond his cottage door
He sprang and gazed, the white hair o'er
His shoulders streaming, and the last
Wild sunset gleam on his worn cheek cast:
He looked and saw his Marion turn
Home from the well beside the burn,
And cried, "Good tidings! Thou and I
Will see our Chief before we die."
That night they talked, how many a year

Had gone, since the last Lochiel was here,
How gentle hearts and brave had been
The old Lochiels their youth had seen;
Aye as they spake, more hotly burned
The fire within them—back returned
Old days seemed ready to revive
That perished in the Forty-five.
That night ere Ewen laid his head
On pillow, to his wife he said:
"Yule-time is near, for many a year
Mirth-making through the glens hath ceased,
But the clan once more, as in days of yore,
Shall hold this Yule with game and feast."

IX

Next morning, long ere screech o' day,
Old Ewen roused hath ta'en the brae
With gun on shoulder, and the boy,
Companion of his toils and joy,
The dark-haired Angus by his side—
O'er the black braes o' Glen Kinzie, on
Among the mists with slinging stride
They fare, nor stayed till they had won
Corrie-na-Gaul, the cauldron deep
Which the Lochiels were used to keep
A sanctuary where the deer might hide,
And undisturbed all year abide.

Not a cranny, rock, or stone
In that corrie but was known
To my grandsire's weird grey eye;
All the lairs where large stags lie
Well he knew, but passed them by,
For stags were lean ere yule-time grown.
Crawling on, he saw appear
O'er withered fern one twinkling ear—
His gun is up—the crags resound—
Startled, a hundred antlers bound
Up the passes fast away;
Lifeless stretched along the ground,
Large and sleek, one old hind lay.
Straight they laid her on their backs,
And o'er the hills between them bore,
Up and down by rugged tracks,
Sore-wearied, ere beside their door
They laid her down—"A bonny beast
To crown our coming yule-time feast"—
As night came down on scour[1] and glen,
From rough Scour-hoshi-brachcalen.

X

That night they slept the slumber sound
That waits on labour long and sore;
Next day he sent the message round

[1] *Scour*, high projecting rock.

The glen from door to door,
On to the neighbouring glens—Glenpean
The summons hears, and all that be in
Glen Kinzie's bounds—Loch Arkaig, stirred
From shore to shore the call has heard;
To Clunes it passed, from toun to toun,[1]
That all the people make them boun [2]
Against the coming New-Year's-Day,
To gather for a shinty fray[3]
Within the long Glen Desseray,
And meet at night round Ewen's board,
In honour of Lochiel restored.

XI

Blue, frosty, bright, the morning rose
That New Year's day above the snows,
Veiling the range of Scour and Ben,
That either side wall in the glen.
But down on the Strath the night frost keen
Had only crisped the long grass green,
When the men of Loch Arkaig, boat and oar
At Kinloch leaving, sprang to shore.
Crisp was the sward beneath their tread
As they westward marched, and at their head
The Piper of Achnacarry blew

[1] *Toun*, farm, or township.
[2] *Boun*, ready.   [3] *Shinty fray*, see Note at end.

The thrilling pibroch of Donald Dhu.
That challenge the Piper of the Glen
As proudly sounded back again
From his biggest pipe, till far off rang
The tingling crags to the wild war-clang
Of the pibroch that loud to battle blown
The Cameron clan had for ages known.
To-day, as other, yet the same,
It summons to the peaceful game;
From the braeside homes down trooping come
The champions of Glen Desseray, some
In tartan philabegs arrayed—
The garb which tyrant laws forbade,
But still they clung to, unafraid;
Some in home-woven tartan trews,
Rough spun, and dyed with various hues,
By mother's hands or maiden's wrought,
In hues by native fancy taught;
But all with hazel camags[1] slung
Their shoulders o'er, men old and young,
With mountaineer's long slinging pace,
Move cheerily down to the trysting-place.

XII

Yonder a level space of ground—
Two miles and more from west to east,

[1] *Camag*, the Gaelic for a club.—J. C. S.

Where from rough Màm-Clach-Ard released
In loop¹ on loop the river wound,
Through many a slow and lazy round,
Ere plunging downward to the lake.
On that long flat of green they take
Their stations; on the west the men
Of Desseray, Kinzie, Pean Glen,
Ranged 'gainst the stalwart lads who bide
Down long Loch Arkaig, either side.
The ground was ta'en, the clock struck ten,
As Ewen, patriarch of the glen,
Struck off, and sent the foremost ball
Down the Strath flying, with a cry;
"Fye, lads, set on," and one and all
To work they fell right heartily.

XIII

Now fast and furious on they drive,—
Here youngsters scud with feet of wind,
There in a melee dunch² and strive;
The veterans outlook keep behind.
Now up, now down, the ball they toss;
Now this, now that side of the Strath;
And many a leaper, brave to cross
The river, finds a chilling bath;

---

¹ *Loop*, see Note at end.
² *Dunch*, swing and plunge forward.

And many a fearless driver bold,
To win renown, was sudden rolled
　　Headlong in hid quagmire;
And many a stroke of stinging pain
In the close press was given and ta'en
　　Without or guile or ire.
So all the day the clansmen played,
And to and fro their tulzie[1] swayed,
Untired, along the hollow vale,
And neither side could win the hail;[2]
But high the clamour, upward flung,
Along the precipices rung,
And smote the snowy peaks, and went
Far up the azure firmament.
All day, too, watching from the knowes,
Stood maidens fair, with snooded brows,
　　And bonny blithe wee bairns;
Those watching whom I need na say,
These eyeing now their daddies play,
　　Now jinking[3] round the cairns.

XIV

The loud game fell with sunset still,
And echo died on strath and hill;
As gloamin' deepened, each side the glen,

---

[1] *Tulzie,* scuffle.　　　　[2] *Hail,* goal.
[3] *Jinking,* turning and darting to escape being caught.

High above the homes of men,
Blinks of kindling fires were seen,
Such as shine out upon Hallowe'en;
Single fires on rocky shelf
Each several farm-house for itself
Has lighted—there in wavering line
Either side the vale they shine
From dusk to dawn, to blaze and burn
In welcome of their Chief's return.
But broader, brighter than the rest,
   Down beside Loch-Arkaig-head,
From a knoll's commanding crest
   One great beacon flaring red,
As with a wedge of splendour clove
The blackness of the vault above.
And far down the quivering waters flung
   Forward its steady pillar of light,
To tell, more clear than trumpet tongue,
   Glen Desseray hails her Chief to-night.

XV

The while the bonfires blazed without,
   With logs and peats by keen hands fed—
Children and men—a merry rout;
   In every home the board was spread.
On ev'ry hearth the fires burned clear,
And round and round abundant cheer

Passed freely for the men who came
From distant glens to join the game.
Freely that feast flowed—most of all
In the old home at Sheneval;
There Ewen Cameron, seated high,
  Welcomed a various company.
Flower of the glens—old men, his peers,
White with the snows of seventy years;
And clansmen, strong in middle age,
And sprightly youths in life's first stage—
Down to his own bright dark-haired boy,
Who, seated in a chimney nook,
  To his inmost bosom took
The impress of that night of joy.

XVI

He feasted them with the venison fine
Himself had brought from Corrie-na-Gaul,
And sent around the ruddy wine,
  High spiced, in antique bowl—
Rare wine, which to the Western Isles
  Ships of France in secret bore,
Thence through Skye and o'er the Kyles,
  Brought to the mainland shore.
Far back that night their converse ran
To the old glories of the clan;
The battles, where in mortal feud

Clan Cameron 'gainst Clan Chattan stood ;
And great Sir Ewen, huge of frame,
'Mid loyal hearts the foremost name,
How, yet a boy, he gave his heart
To the King's cause and great Montrose ;
How hand to hand, in tangled den
He closed with Cromwell's staunchest men,
And conqueror from the death-grips rose :
How the war-summons of Dundee
In hoary age he sprang to meet—
Dashed with his clan in headlong charge
Down Killiecrankie's cloven gorge
To victory deadlier than defeat.
At these old histories inly burned
The heart of Ewen—back returned
The vigour of long-vanished years,
A youth he stood 'mid hoary peers.
Even as in autumn you have seen
Some ancient pine alone look green
   'Mid all the wasted wood's decay ;
Some pine, that having summer long
Repaired its verdure, fresh and strong
   Waits the bleak winter day.

XVII

As Ewen's spirit caught the glow
Cast from the heights of long ago,

His own old memories became
Within his heart a living flame;
And, bursting the reserve that long
Had kept them down, broke forth in song.

1

"What an August morn that was!
    Think na' ye our hearts were fain,[1]
Branking down the Cuernan Pass,
    To Glenfinnan's trysting-plain;

2

"Where the glen lies open,—where
    Spread the blue waves of Loch Shiel—
Lealest hearts alone were there,
    Keppoch, Moidart, brave Lochiel;

3

"There was young Clanranald true—
    Crowding all round Scotland's Heir—
Him, the Lad with bonnet blue
    And the long bright yellow hair.

4

"Kingly look that morn he wore
    In our Highland garb arrayed,
By his side the broad claymore,
    O'er his brow the white cockade,

---

[1] *Fain*, eager.

5
Well I ween, he looked with pride
   On that gathering by Loch Shiel,
As while the veteran, old and tried,
   Tullibardine, true as steel,

6
"On the winds with dauntless hand
   Flung the crimson flag unfurled,
Pledge that we to death would stand
   For the Stuarts 'gainst the world.

7
"Jeanie Cameron gazed apart,
   Where our people crowned the brae,
Proudly beat her gallant heart
   At the sight of that brave day.

8
"Loud the shouting shakes the earth,
   Far away the mountains boom,
As the Chiefs and Clansmen forth
   March to victory and to doom."

The while he sang, in fervent dream
The old man's eye beheld the gleam
Of yet another Forty-five
Along those western shores revive,
And Moidart mountains re-illume—
The glory, but no more the gloom.

CANTO SECOND

BOTHAIN-AIRIDH; OR, THE SHEALINGS[1]

I

WHEN from copse, and craig, and summit
    Comes the cuckoo's lonely cry
Down the glen from morn to midnight
    Sounding, warm June days are nigh.
At that cry, the heart of Allan
    Turns towards the shealings green,
Where for ages every summer
    Men of Sheaniebhal have been.
Bonny shealings, green and bielded,[2]
    Where there meet two corrie burns,
Ault-na-noo and Ault-a-bhealaich,
    Pouring from high mountain urns.
Small green knolls of pasture fringing
    Skirts of darksome Màm-clach-ard,
Scour-na-naat and Scour-na-ciecha
    Westward keeping aweful guard.
Allan then, one grave glance round him
    East and west the long glen cast,

---

[1] *Shealings*, summer grazing high on the hills; also, shepherd's huts, chalets.   [2] *Bielded*, sheltered.

Saw the clouds were high and steady,
   Knew the wintry weather was past;
Then spake loud to all his people—
   " Mak' ye for the shealings boun :"
On the morrow every door was
   Closed within the old farm-toun.

II

When the light lay on the mountains
   Of a morning calm and mild,
From their homes the people going
   Set their faces to the wild.
Then were seen whole families climbing
   Up among the hoary cairns,
Grandsires, grandames, fathers, mothers,
   Lads and lasses, winsome bairns,
Driving calves, and kye for milking,
   Goats and small sheep on before,
Two white ponies trudging after
   With their all of household store.
Here the blackcock, all his rivals
   Driven aloof, on yonder mound
Sits and spreads his snowy pinion,
   Drumming to his mates around.
There the redcock, new in plumage,
   Scarlet crest in fresh May-glow,
From the distant heights replying,

Calls aloud with cheery crow.
Yonder Alpine hare before them
    Canters lazily away,
With her coat snow-white in winter,
    Now returned to dark-blue grey;
Then aloof, on hind legs rising,
    Perking ears in curious mood,
Listens, " whence have these intruders
    Come to scare my solitude?"
Downward the hen-harrier stooping,
    To and fro doth flit and wheel,
Stealthily along the heather,
    Hunting for his morning meal.

III

Westward sloped the sun, ere reaching
    Hillocks by the meeting burns,
Men begin last summer's bothies
    Thatching, with dry heath and ferns.
Wives the while, small ingles kindle,
    Spread fresh heather beds on floor;
For the milk and cheese make ready
    Roomy sconce in ben-most bore.[1]
Angus and his kilted comrades
    In the hill-burn plash and shout,
All about the granite boulders

---

[1] *Sconce*, shelter: *Ben-most bore*, innermost corner.

Guddling[1] for the speckled trout.
Well-a-day! but life was bonny
   With our folk in those old days;
Children barefoot, morn and even,
   Wandering high on brackeny braes;
Lips and faces purpled over
   With the rich abundant fill
Of blae, wortle, and crow-berries,
   Gathered wide from craig and hill;
Nature's own free gladness sharing
   Through the sweetest of the year,
With the red grouse crowing round them,
   And far-heard the belling deer;
From behind, the mountain quiet
   Blending with the lilting cry
Of the women homeward calling
   Down their goats and dauted kye.[2]

IV

It befell one time of shealings
   Allan with his youngest boy,
Angus, high above the bothies
   Wandered on some hill-employ;
When from top of Ault-a-bhealaich
   Looking, they beheld the bowl,

---

[1] *Guddling,* groping.
[2] *Dauted kye,* favourite, doated-on cattle.

Caldron-shaped and dark in shadow,
  Far beneath, of Corrie-na-Gaul.
" Was not that the hiding-place," cried
  Angus, starting at the name,
" Where ye refuged, when Prince Charlie
  Guiding, through these hills ye came ?"
" Many a place we had for hiding,"
  Answered Allan, " first and last :"
" Tell me all the way ye travelled,
  Whence the Prince came, whither passed."
" Well, dear laddie ! sith ye will it,
  I will teach thee what befell
After that the Prince bade Flora,
  And the shores of Skye farewell.

V

" As he steered up dark Loch Nevish,
  And set foot on mainland shore,
Deadly foes were close behind him,
  Deadly, keeping watch before.
Seaward, every frith and islet,
  Girt and swept by hostile sail ;
Landward, one long line of sentries,
  Post on post, kept hill and dale.
High and low, on glen and summit,
  From Glenfinnan to Lochourn,
All the day saw guards patrolling,

All the night red watch-fires burn.
Fast across the hills of Morar
   Sped the Prince to Borrodale—
That leal House, when first he landed,
   Welcomed him with glad 'all hail.'
There before his eyes the bonny
   Homestead lay—a blackened heap—
Mid the craigs and woods o'erhanging,
   The old Laird in hiding deep
With his sons kept. Thither guided,
   Lay the Prince in safety there
For three days, till foemen prowling
   Close and closer girt their lair.
Then these leal Macdonalds longer
   Could not their loved Prince conceal,
He must leave Clanranald's country
   For the mountains of Lochiel.
Soon to Cameron of Glenpean
   Came the word that he must wait
For the Prince, on one lone hill, and
   Guide him through that desperate strait.
To our toun, came Donald crying,
   'Up and help the Prince with me,'
For he knew of these hill-passes
   I had better skill than he.

VI

"Long we kept the cairn of trysting,
    But none living came that way;
Then to seek them through the mountains
    Far we wandered: summer day
Into midnight deep was darkening,
    When low down faint forms appear,
Through a slack[1] between the mountains
    Moving dim like straggling deer.
Who they might be, all unknowing,
    Down we hurried to the vale;
Forward one then stept to meet us—
    Who but brave Glenaladale?
Glad was he to find no stranger,
    But Glenpean, whom he knew;
Glad the Prince to greet a Cameron
    Long since proven leal and true.
Two days after dark Culloden,
    A night 'neath Donald's roof he lay,
When in haste for Moidart making
    Came he by Loch Arkaig way.

VII

"'Come, thrice welcome! fain are we to
    Place our lives within thy hand,

---

[1] *Slack*, opening between two hills.

Through these fires, where'er you lead us,
    We will follow thy command,'
Low the Prince to Donald whispered,
    For the watch-fires blazed anear,
And the sentry-voices answering,
    Each to other, smote our ear.
' Trust us, Prince ! our best endeavour
    We will give to bring you through,
But the paths are rough and rocky,
    And the hours of darkness few.'
Then, as leaders, I and Donald
    On thro' darkness groped and crawled,
Down black moss-hags [1] gashed and miry,
    Up great corries, torrent-scrawled ;
Till all faint with toil and travel,
    As around the watch-fires wane,
In the first grey of the dawning
    Yonder summit we attain,—
Southern wall of long Glen Desseray,
    Mamnyn-Callum—that round hill—
There, like hares far-hunted, squatting
    Close we kept all day and still ;
Eyeing the red-coats beneath us,
    How like wasps they swarm and spread
From their camp within the meadow,
    Pitched beside Loch-Arkaig-head.

[1] *Moss-hags*, pits or gashes in a boggy moor.

Though so near, Glenpean bade the
    Prince take rest, and nothing dread,
For yestreen all Mamnyn-Callum
    They had searched from base to head.

VIII

" Sundown over Scour-na-ciecha,
    Forth we creep from out our lair,
Just as the watch-fires rekindling
    Leap up through the gloamin' air.
On the face of Meal-na-Sparden,
    'Neath the sentries close, we keep
Westward, down yon cliff descending
    To Glen-Lochan-Anach deep.
At the darkest of the night, we
    Crossed our own Glen-head, and heard
Eerie voices of the howlets
    Hooting from dim Màm-clach-ard.
Crawling then, up Ault-a-bhealaich,
    Just at this spot—waning dim
O'er the mountains of Glengarry—
    Ghost-like hung the crescent's rim.
When we turned the bealach,[1] downward
    By yon rocky rough burn-head;
With this right hand, through the darkness
    Him, our darling Prince, I led.

[1] *Bealach*, narrow pass.

O ! to think that such as I should
    Grasp within this hand of mine
Him, the heir of all these Islands,
    Last of Albyn's kingly line !
Think that he was fain to refuge
    In yon grim and dripping hold ;
He whose home should hae been a palace,
    And his bed a couch of gold !

IX

"All these gnarl'd black-corried mountains
    Hold no den like Corrie-na-Gaul—
Womb of blackest rain-storms—cradle
    Of the winds, that fiercest howl.
See ye yon grey rocky screetan [1]
    Down from that dark precipice strown,
There I led them to a cavern
    Under yon huge shelter-stone.
All the day we heard the gun-shots
    On the mountains overhead,
Well we knew red-coats were busy
    Shooting our poor people dead.
Two days we had all but fasted,
    Now were growing hunger-faint,
All the while the Prince would cheer us,

---

[1] *Screetan*, stony ravine, track of torrent, or stony debris on mountain-side.

Not one murmur or complaint;
Though for many days, the choicest
　　Fare he had his want to fill
Was scant oatmeal, cold spring water,
　　And wild berries from the hill.
So in search of food I ventured
　　Down to where some shealings were,
But I found them all abandoned,
　　And the bothies empty and bare.
Baffled, I returned and brought them
　　Forth from our dark cavern-bed,
And, though full the daylight, led them
　　Warily to a mountain head,
That o'erlooked Glen-quoich's dark waters;
　　There, what saw we close below
But a camp with red-coats swarming,
　　And a troop in haste to go
Up the very hill we lodged in?
　　All about they searched that day,
Close we cowered, and heaven so guided
　　That they came not where we lay.
Then the Prince said, 'Not another
　　Sun shall rise ere we shall make
Trial to pass the chain of sentries—
　　Life upon that hazard stake.'

X

"Gloamin' fell, we rose and started
    From our lair, a stealthy race
O'er that stream and flat Lōn-meadow,
    Up yon wrinkled mountain face,—
Druim-a-chosi,—from that summit
    Seen, a watch-fire wildly burned
In the glen, across our pathway—
    Westward to the side we turned:
And so close we passed it, voices
    Of the sentinels reached our ear—
Low we crouched, and round the hillocks
    Crawled, like stalkers of the deer.
Up a hill flank—(Druim-a-chosi
    Will not let us now discern)
Scrambling up a torrent's bed, we
    Won the ridge of Leach-na-fearn.
There, in our descending pathway
    Down before us, full in view
Watch-fires twain in grey dawn flickered,
    That way we must venture through.
Then I said, 'Prince! ere you venture,
    Let me first the passage prove;'
And, with that, few steps to westward
    Crept adown a torrent's groove.
There I watched till warders pacing
    Passed each other, back to back;

Swift, but mute, I passed between them,
    Safe returned the self-same track.
And we all kept close in shelter,
    Till again they face to face
Met and passed each other, leaving,
    Back to back, an empty space.
Quick I darted forward, whispering,
    'Now's our time, Prince! follow me:'
Few brief breathless moments crawling
    Down the corrie [1]—we were free.
Out beyond the chain of sentries,
    Down by Lochan-doire-dhu,
'Neath the bield [2] of birks and alders,
    Past the mouth of Corrie-hoo,
Up the rock of Innis-craikie—
    Just as the last star grew pale
On the brow of Scour-a-vorrar,
    Reached we Corrie-scorridale.

XI

"There, in rocky den safe-sheltered,
    O the welcome blest repose!
Time at last for food and slumber,
    Respite from relentless foes.
When a day and night were over,
    We arose and wandered on,

---

[1] *Corrie*, see note, p. 7.   [2] *Bield*, shelter.

Northward to the Seaforth country,
  West from long Glenmorriston.
Then, I knew my work was ended,
  For those hills to me were strange,
And a clansman of Glengarry's
  Bred amid that mountain range—
One who had shar'd Culloden battle—
  Was at hand a guide to be.
Then the Prince turned round, and gazing
  On my face, spake words to me:
'Allan! what can I repay thee
  For thy service done so well?
Naught but thanks are mine to render,
  Heart-deep thanks, and long farewell.'
In his own he grasped this right hand,
  The Prince grasped it—never since—
Never while I breathe shall mortal
  Grasp this hand which touched the Prince.[1]
Think na ye the tears came fa'ing,
  Think na ye my heart was sair,
Watching him depart, and knowing
  I should see his face nae mair."

[1] See Note at end.

GLEN DESSERAY, OR

CANTO THIRD

"ON THE TRACK OF THE PRINCE"

I

DOWN to Loch Nevish went the day,
And all that night young Angus lay
'Tween dream and waking,—heart on fire
With inextinguishable desire
To trace each step the Prince had gone
From Morar to Glengarry,—on,
O'er rifted peak, and cove profound,
Exploring every inch of ground,
Until he reached the famed ravine
Through which he passed the guards between;
For every spot the Prince had trode
To him with sacred radiance glowed.

II

When the first streaks of morning broke
Above Glengarry mountains, woke
Young Angus from his heather bed,
Stole through the bothy door, and said
No word to any of the way
Him listed take that summer day.

THE SEQUEL OF CULLODEN

Up by the Ault-a-bhealaich burn
Lightly he went, and at the turn
Of waters, plunged down Corrie-na-Gaul,—
That dark cavernous cauldron-bowl,
O'er-canopied, morn and eve, with mist,—
Therein he sought the cave he wist
His father pointed out yestreen
Where he erewhile with the Prince had been.
Thence down the corrie-burn he bore,
And up on precipiced Scour-a-vhor
Sought where they refuged.   Then in haste
He hurried o'er the low wide waste,—
The Lōn, o'er which the wanderers ran
That night, when their last march began
To pass the sentries ; then he hied
Up Druimahoshi's rugged side ;
But on his spirit solemn awe
Fell when, the summit won, he saw
To westward Knoydart peaks up-crowd,
Scarred, jagg'd, black-corried—some in cloud,
Some by slant sunbursts glory-kissed,—
Beyond—through fleeces broad of mist
   Like splintered spears weird peaks of Skye,
And many an isle he could not name,
That looming into vision came
   From ocean's outer mystery.

III

Long Angus stood and gazed, and when,
Downward, he searched the farther glen,
The westering sun toward ocean bending
From the hill edge slant rays was sending
Backward o'er gnarled Scour-a-chlive,
And greener flanks of Leach-na-fern.
Well Angus knew the Prince had passed
The guards up there, and keenly cast
His eyes all over them to discern
Some crevice in their mountain wall
Up which the wanderer's feet could crawl.

IV

Three burns there are, as I have seen,
Poured from that hill-side—one between
Scour-a-chlive and Leach-na-fern,
Called of the people the March-burn,
Because its channel doth divide
Rough Knoydart from Glengarry side:
And one, Ault-Scouapich, that doth leap,—
The Besom burn—down the middle steep;
   Westmost of all a stream that drains
The severed peaks of Scour-a-chlive,
   Called from old time the Burn of brains,
Through the rough hill-flank down doth drive

A deep indented furrow, till,
The level reached, within a still
Small meadowy spot, that greenly gleams
Amid the waste, made glad with streams,
That hill-burn, loop on loop, entwined
Goes wandering gently down, to find
The great Glen-river. Of these three
Which might the very channel be
By which the Prince passed upward, no
Foot-print or sign remains to show.
So to himself young Angus said,
 As o'er and o'er with eager ken
From left to right his eyes surveyed
 The northern steep that walls the glen.

V

Wearied and baffled with the quest
 All day pursued in vain,
His eyes went wandering east and west
To corrie and scaur, in blank unrest,
 Again and yet again.
O'er earth our mightiest movements pass,
 And leave no deeper impress than
Cloud-shadows on the mountain grass,
 So fleeting and so frail is man.
The Princely feet that mountain wall
Passed over, but have left no scrawl;

This desert saw what here befell
But hath no voice or sign to tell,
And the rocks keep their secret well.
As thoughts like these athwart him swept
Fain had he sat him down and wept.

VI

But day was westering, and the cloud
Down on the glooming summits bowed
Brought o'er his heart a sudden fear
Of night in that lone place austere.
Then he arose in haste, and clomb
   The steep in panting hope to win
On the other side some human home,
   Or even some cave to shelter in.
Soon as he crossed the highest cope,
He saw, cleaving the northern slope,
A birchen corrie with its burn
Now bare, now hidden. "Thou my turn
Wilt serve," he cried; "with thee for guide,
I'll go where'er thy waters glide."
Soon as his eager footstep trode
Beside it, on the grassy sod,
The pleasant murmur in his ear
Was like a voice of human cheer,
And seemed to lift away the load
That all day long had overawed

And weighed his spirit down with stress
Of too prevailing loneliness:
Lightly he trode down Corriebeigh,
The burn companion of his way,
Now by the greensward winding, gliding,
Now in the birchen coppice hiding,
Then plunging forward and chafing far
Underneath some crumbling scaur,
Anon in daylight re-appearing
To greet him with a sound of cheering,
Till it reached far down in a glimmering pass
A little lochan,[1] marged with grass:
He watched the small burn steal therein
And rest for its wandering water win,
And the thought arose within his breast,
" Haply I too may here find rest."

VII

Then turning round, small space aloof,
   Under a bield of the birchen wood,
He saw a bothy of wicker woof
With bracken and heather for its roof,
   Like lair of wild beast, rough and rude.
A moment's space, he paused before
The opening dark that seemed a door,
And gazed around,—indistinct and dim

[1] *Lochan*, small lake.

The black crags vague in vapour swim;
Naught clear in all the glimmering pass
But the lochan-gleam with its marge of grass,
And the flash of the great white waterfall
Down thundering from the northern wall,
And filling with o'eraweing roar
The solemn pass forevermore.
No time to look or listen long,
    Ere forth there stept from the bothy door
An old man, tall, erect, and strong—
    Threescore years he had seen or more,—
Survivor of the Forty-five,
    One of the old Glengarry clan,
Who wont not from his lair to drive
    Any wandering man;
He kindly welcomed Angus in,
Unquestioning of his home or kin.

VIII

But when the lad, with bashful face,
Told how he came to that lone place,
That he had wandered since break of day
From the shealings of Glen Desseray,
One of Lochiel's own people—son
Of veteran Ewen Cameron—
At hearing of that well-known name
Murdoch Macdonnell's cheek like flame

Brightened, and in his hand he took
The lad's, and to the ingle-nook
Of the bothy led him, saying aloud,
"Son of my battle friend, how proud
Am I to bid thee welcome here;
For him thy Sire, true man sincere.
Years have gone by, since we two met,
   Like me, he must be touched with eld,
But till the Gael their Prince forget
   In honour will his name be held."

IX

Upon the settle seated, o'er
That ancient tale they went once more,
And Murdoch told the very place—
The burn that grooves the southern face
Of Leach-na-fern—where Angus led
The Prince across the watershed,
Thence through the sentinels crept their way,
Down the clefts of this same Corriebeigh.
Anon his board the old man piled
With the best increase of the wild—
Red-spotted trout, fresh from the stream,
   Hill-berries, stored in autumn hours,
And goat-milk cheese, and yellow cream
   Rich with the juice of mountain flowers:
And oatmeal cake and barley scone,—

Sweet viands for a hungry guest
To break his day-long fast upon,
Before he sought his couch of rest.
That couch old Murdoch's hands had spread
With the fresh crop of heather green
Turned upward—never prince, I ween,
On easier pillow laid his head.
Though soft the bed, and the rough way
Had wearied him, yet Angus lay
Far into night, through the still gloom
Listening the sleepless cataract boom,
In busy thought back-wandering through
The lonely places, strange and new,
That day had to his sight revealed,
Ere slumber soft his eyelids sealed.

CANTO FOURTH

THE HOME BY LOCHOURN

I

Early young Angus rose to meet
The morning. Glimmering at his feet—
There lay the lochan, clear as glass,
The margin green with reeds and grass,
Within the lap of the awesome pass,
That from Glengarry's westmost bourne
Breaks headlong down on lone Lochourn.
Over the shoulder of the world
The sun looked, and the pale mists curled
On black crag-faces, smit to gold,
And rose and lingered, crept and rolled
Up the ravines and splintered heights,
All beautiful with the dawning lights.
A pleasant morn it was of June,
 The time of year that most awakes
The mountain melodists to tune
 Their sweetest songs from heaths and brakes;
The mavis' voice rang from the copse,
 Upon his knoll the blackcock crowed,
And up toward the bare hill-tops

The cuckoo shouted loud.
Across the deep gorge, under all
Kept sounding on the torrent fall,
That thundering down with sleepless wave
We Gael call Essan-corrie-Graive.

II

Soon as the early meal was o'er,
Murdoch looked from the bothy door,
And said, " I go to Lochourn's lone side,
   Where my bairns in our winter home delay;
Wilt thither go with me, and bide
   Beneath my roof one other day?
To-morrow, my Ronald shall be thy guide
   Over the hills to Glen Desseray."
Westward they went with morning joy,
That old man and light-hearted boy:
Ah! beautiful the mountain road
As ever foot of mortal trode,
Winding west through the cloven defile
Of crags fantastic, pile on pile,
Towering rock, huge boulder stone,
Heather-crowned and lichen-grown,
And crumpled mountain walls, ravined
With birchen-corries, sunlight-sheened,
Where the torrent plunged and flashed in spray
Down to the little lochans that lay

Gleaming in the lap of the Pass
Fringed with reeds, and marged with grass.
As they the early day beguile
Sauntering through the long defile,
Upon young Angus' wondering sense
With new-born beauty, power intense,
Of craig and scaur, of copse and dell
And far-off peaks the vision fell;
All seemed endued, he knew not how,
With glory never seen till now.

III

At length old Murdoch silence broke,
And Angus from his dream awoke,—
"Ye see that slack[1] on the water-shed;
That was the way your Father led
Our noble Prince the sentinels through;
Then down by this same Corrie-hoo
They came, and crossed our path just here,
And round the end of yon small mere,
Up through that hazel wood they went,
Over yon rocky sheer ascent,
And reached, as the last star grew pale,
The Cave of Corrie-scorridale;
And there—I've heard your Father tell—
He bade the Prince a long farewell."

[1] *Slack*, see note, p. 28.

IV

Then round a rock a sudden turn
Showed far below deep-walled Lochourn—
Blue inlet from the distant seas
   Piercing far up the mountain world;
In the calm noon no breath or breeze
   Along the azure waters curled.
At sight thereof their sense was smote
With fresh sea-savour; though remote
From the main ocean many a mile
Inflooded past cape, creek, and kyle,[1]
The sea-loch, flanked by precipice walls,
With ever-lessening murmur crawls,
Till 'neath the Pass he lies subdued
By the o'eraweing solitude;
And yet some vigour doth retain,
Some freshness of the parent main.

V

So have I seen it: many a day
Is gone since last I passed that way,
Yet still in memory lives impressed
The image of its aweful rest.
The winds there wont to work their will
That day were quiet—all was still,

---

[2] *Kyle*, sound or strait.

Save that one headlong cataract hoar
From steep Glenelg's opposing shore
Sent o'er the loch a lulling sound,
That made the hush but more profound.
There in clear mirror imaged lay
The lichened cliffs tall, silver-grey,
Their ledges interlaced with green;
 The cataract of white-sheeted spray
Down flashing through the dark ravine,
 The birches clambering up midway
The sea-marge and hill-tops between;
Each herb, each floweret, tiny-leaved,
Into that lucid depth received,
Therein repeated, hue and line,
With more than their own beauty shine,
Embedded in a nether sky,
More fairy-fleeced than that on high:
A scene it seemed of beauty and peace,
So deep it could not change or cease.

VI

Through such a scene, on such a day,
 They wandered down that lovely noon,
Now 'neath high headlands making way
 Among huge blocks at random strewn;
Now round some gentle bay they wind,
Green nook, with golden shingle lined,

Whither the weary fisher oars
His boat for mooring ; then by doors
They went, of kindly crofter-folk,
Whence many a gladsome greeting broke ;
And Murdoch told them, now was time
To the high shealings they should climb ;
Himself there with his goats had been
And seen the pastures growing green.
To-morrow he and his would drive
   Their ponies and sheep, and bonny kine,
Up to the back of Scour-a-chlaive,
   Where the springs ran clear and the grass
      was fine :
And there the clansmen would forgather
All in the pleasant bright June weather ;
So he warned the Lochside, toun by toun,
To make them for the shealings boune.

VII

The day had westered far, and on
The yellow pines the sunset shone,
Streamed back from Lurvein, kindling them
To redder lustre, branch and stem,
Ere they reached the pine-tree on the crown
   Sole-standing of the promontory,
Whence they beheld far-gazing down
   The loch inlaid with sunset glory.

Long time beside that sole pine-tree
They stood and gazed in ecstasy,
For the face of heaven was all a-glow
    With molten splendour backward streamed
From the sunken sun, and the loch below,
    Flushed with an answering glory, gleamed.
Each purple cloud aloft that burned
In the depth below was back returned.
There headlands, each o'erlapping each,
Projecting down the long loch's reach,
With point of rock and plume of pine,
All glorious in the sunset shine :
And far down on the verge of sight
    Rock-islets interlacing lie,
That lapt in floor of molten light
    Seemed natives less of earth than sky.
From height of heaven to ocean bed
One living splendour penetrated,
And made that moment seem to be
Bridal of earth and sky and sea.

VIII

As died away the wondrous glow,
They wandered down to a home below;
A little home, where the mountain burn,
    Thrown from the pine-crags, touched the
        shore :

There waiting for their Sire's return
   His family meet him at the door ;
His own wife, Marion, hail and leal,[1]
Just risen from her humming wheel,
Their eldest—Donald,—nearing now
   The verge of manhood, hunter keen ;
And Ronald, with the open brow
   And bright eye-glance of blithe sixteen.
And his one daughter, loved so well,
The dark-haired, blue-eyed Muriel.
These all were waiting, fain to know
How soon they might to the shealing go ;
And while much-wondering whence the boy,
To whom their Sire had been convoy,
They made him welcome with their best
Beneath their roof that night to rest.
There in that beautiful retreat
Companions young and converse sweet
Woke Angus to another mood
Than he had nursed in solitude.
No more by cave and mountain-slack
He dreamed o'er the lorn Prince's track ;
Those weary wanderings all forgot
Were changed for fields of happier thought,
And fairer visions, fresh with dew
Of a dream-land not old but new.

   [1] *Hail and leal*, healthy and faithful.

CANTO FIFTH

THE WAR SUMMONS

I

Soon as the kindling dawn had tipt
   With gold Scour-vorrar's lonely head,
Before a single ray had dipt
   Down to the loch's deep-shadowed bed,
Betimes old Marion was astir,
Thinking of that young wanderer,
And eident [1] fitly to prepare
For all the household morning fare.
That over, Murdoch rose and went
Up through the pines, the steep ascent,
His two lads with him, to convoy
Homeward the wandering Cameron boy.
From the high peaks soon they showed a track,
That followed on would lead him back
To where his people's shealings lay,
On heights above Glen Desseray;
Then bade farewell—but ere they part
The three lads vowed with eager heart
That they, ere long, with willing feet,
Would hasten o'er the hills to meet.

[1] *Eident*, diligent.

II

Many a going and return
Down to lone, beautiful Lochourn,
That pathway witnessed—many a time
These young lads crossed it, fain to climb
Each to the other's shealings, there
The pastimes of the hills to share—
To fish together the high mere,
Track to his lair the straggling deer,
From refuge in the cairn of rocks
Unearth the lamb-destroying fox;
Or creep, with balanced footing nice,
  Where o'er some awful chasm hung,
On ledge of dripping precipice,
  The brooding eagle rears her young.
So from that wild, free nurture grew
'Tween these three lads firm friendship true.
  But most the soul of Ronald clave
To Angus, his own chosen friend—
  To Angus more than brother gave
Tender affection without end—
Such as young hearts give in their prime—
  A weight of love, no lesser than
The love wherewith, in that old time,
  David was loved by Jonathan.

III

At length the loud war-thunder broke
O'er Europe, and the land awoke,
Even to the innermost recess
Of this far-western wilderness.
And the best councillors of the Crown—
They who erewhile had hunted down
Our sires on their own mountains, now,
Led by a wiser man, 'gan trow
'Twere better and more safe to use
Our good claymores and hardy thews
'Gainst Britain's foes, than shoot us dead,
Food for the hill-fox and the glead.[1]
To all the Chieftains of the North
An edict from the King went forth,
That who should to his standard bring
   From his own hills a stalwart band
Of clansmen in his following,
   Himself should lead them and command.
He could not hear—our own Lochiel—
With heart unmoved that strong appeal,
To rouse once more the ancient breed
   Of warriors, as his sires had done,
And help his country in her need
   With the flower of brave Clan Cameron.

[1] *Glead*, kite.

IV

Then every morning Achnacarry
Saw clansmen mustering in hot hurry—
Saw every glen that owns Lochiel,
    Lochaber Braes, and all Màm-more,
Glenluy, west to fair Loch Shiel,
    Their bravest to the trysting pour.
Westward the summons passed, as flame
    By shepherds lit, some dry March day,
Sweeps over heathery braes—so came
    The tidings to Glen Desseray;
And found the men of Shenebhal
Down in the meadow, busy all
Their stacks of barley set to bind,
Against the winter's rain and wind:
All the flower of the Glen—
Grown, or nearly grown to men—
Heard that summons, all between
Thirty years and bright eighteen,
Loth or willing, slow or fleet,
Rose their Chieftain's call to meet;
Angus, youngest, eager most
To join the quickly mustering host.
Though sad his sire, he could but feel
His boy must follow young Lochiel,
And his mother's heart, tho' wae,

Did not dare to say him nay.
When the following morn appeared,
Down the loch their boat they steered
To Achnacarry, there to enrol
Their names upon the muster-scroll,
And receive their Chief's command,
    To gather when a month was gone,
And follow to a foreign land
    The young heir of Clan Cameron.

V

What were they doing by Lochourn,
    At the Farm of Rounieval,
When there came that sudden turn
    To Angus' fortunes, changing all?
The tidings found, at close of day,
Ronald and Muriel on their way
Homeward, by the winding shore,
Driving the cattle on before.
At hearing of that startling word
The heart of Ronald, deeply stirred,
Wrought to and fro—Must I then part
From him, the brother of my heart;
Let him go forth, on some far shore,
To perish, seen of me no more?
It must not be, shall not be so,
Where Angus goeth, I will go.

Soon to his sister's ear he brought
The secret thing that in him wrought—
" I go with Angus—side by side
" We'll meet, whatever fate betide."

VI

Who, that hath ever known the power
Of home, but to life's latest hour
Will bear in mind the deathly knell,
That on his infant spirit fell,
When first some voice, low-whispering said
" One lamb in the home-fold lies dead ;"
Or that drear hour, scarce less forlorn,
When tidings to his ear was borne,
That the first brother needs must part
From the home-circle, heart to heart
Fast bound,—must leave the well-loved place,
Alone the world's bleak road to face.
Then as their hearts strain after him,
With many a prayer and yearning dim,
The old home, they feel, erst so serene,
No more can be as it has been.
Just so that sudden summons fell
Upon the heart of Muriel,
Even like a sudden funeral bell—
An iron knell of deathly doom
To wither all her young life's bloom.

VII

Few words of dool that night they spake,
Though their two hearts were nigh to break,
But with the morrow's purpling dawn
Ronald and Muriel they are gone
Up through the pine-trees, till they clomb
The highest ridge upon the way
That strikes o'er Knoydart mountains from
Lochourn-side to Glen Desseray;
And there they parted. Not, I ween,
Was that their latest parting morn;
Yet seldom have those mountains seen
Two sadder creatures, more forlorn,
Than these two moving, each apart,
To commune with their own lone heart,
To Achnacarry, one to share
The muster of the clansmen there,
And one, all lonely, to return
Back to the desolate, dark Lochourn.
And yet no wild and wayward wail
Went up from bonny Rounieval,
But Muriel set her to prepare
  Against the final parting day,
A tartan plaid for Ronald's wear,
  When he was far away.

She took the has-wool,[1] lock by lock,
 The choice wool, she in summers old,
What time her father sheared his flock,
 Had gathered by the mountain fold.
She washed and carded it clean and fine,
 Then, sitting by the birling [2] wheel,
She span it out, a slender twine,
 And hanked it on the larger reel,
Singing a low, sad chaunt the while,
That might her heavy heart beguile.

VIII

The hanks she steeped in diverse grains—
 Rich grains, last autumn time distilled
By her own hands, with curious pains,
 Learnt from old folk in colours skilled.
Deep dyes of orange, which she drew
 From crotal [3] dark on mountain top,
And purples of the finest hue
 Pressed from fresh heather crop.
Black hues which she had brewed from bark
Of the alders, green and dark,
Which overshadow streams that go,
 After they have won the vale,

---

[1] *Has-wool*, see Note at end.
[2] *Birling*, whirring, rattling.
[3] *Crotal*, a lichen (Omphalodes) now called *Cudbear*.

Seaward winding still and slow,
  Down by gloomy Barrisdale.
Thereto she added diverse juices,
Taken for their colouring uses,
From the lily flowers that float
High on mountain lochs remote;
And yellow tints the tanzy yields,
Growing in forsaken fields—
All these various hues she found
On her native Highland ground.

IX

But besides she fused and wrought
In her chalice tinctures brought
From far-off countries—blue of Ind,
From plants that by the Ganges grew,
And brilliant scarlets, well refined,
From cochineal, the cactus rind
Yields on warm hills of Mexico.
When in these tinctures long had lain
The several hanks, and drank the grain,
She sunned them on the homeside grass,
  Before the door, above the burn,
Then to the weaver's home did pass,
  Who lived to westward, down Lochourn.
She watched the webster while he tried
  Her hanks, and put the dyes to proof,

Then to the loom her fingers tied,
    Just as he bade her, warp and woof,
The threads of bonny haslock woo'—
    Her haslock woo' well dyed and fine,
And she matched the colours, hue with hue,
    Laid them together, line on line.
And as the treddles rattling went,
    And the swift shuttle whistled through,
It seemed as though her heart-strings blent
    With every thread that shuttle drew.

X

When two moons had waxed and waned,
And the third was past the full,
And the weary cup was all but drained
Of long suspense, and naught remained,
But the one day of parting dool,
From Achnacarry Ronald passed
Down to Lochourn, to bid farewell
To father, mother, brother dear,
And his sole sister Muriel.
For word had come the new-raised band,
Ere two days pass must leave their land,
To march on foreign service—where,
Not even their chief could yet declare.
Far had the autumn waned that morn,
When Ronald left his home forlorn,

And all his family rose and went
  Forth by his side to cheer his way,
To the tryst whither he was bent,
  At foot of long Glen Desseray.
And as they went was Muriel wearing
  Around her breast the new-woven plaid,
And Ronald tall, with gallant bearing,
  Walked in clan tartan garb arrayed.
A while they kept the winding shores
Of wan Lochourn—from friendly doors
Many a heartily breathed farewell
On the ears of the passing family fell.
Then up through dark Glen Barrisdale lay
Their path the morning chill and grey,
And drearily the fitful blast
Moaned down the corries, as they passed,
And floated in troops around their head
From withered birks [1] the wan leaves dead;
And the swathes of mist, in the black gulphs curled,
On the gusty breezes swayed and swirled,
Up to the cloud that in solid mass
Roofed the Màm above and the lonely Pass.
Into that cloud the travellers bore—
Lochourn and his islands were seen no more.

[1] *Birks*, birch-trees.

XI

As they passed from the Màm and its cloudy cowl
Beneath lay Loch Nevish with grim, black scowl—
The blackest, sullenest loch that fills
The ocean-rents of these gnarled hills;
Those flanking hills, where evermore
Dank vapours swim, wild rain-floods pour.
Where ends the loch the way is barred
By the awesome pass of Màm-clach-ard,
By some great throes of Nature rent
Between two mountains imminent;
Scour-na-naat with sharp wedge soaring,
Scour-na-ciche, cataracts pouring
From precipice to precipice,
Headlong down many a blind abyss.
A place it was, e'en at noon or morn,
Of dim, weird sights, and sounds forlorn,
But after nightfall, lad nor lass
In all Lochiel would face that pass.
Now as these travellers climb the Màm,
They were aware of a stern, grim calm—
The calm of the autumn afternoon,
When night and storm will be roaring soon.
But little time, I ween, had they
To watch strange shapes, weird sounds to hear,
For they must hasten on their way—

Not feed on phantasies of fear,
Lest night should fall on them before
They reached Loch Arkaig's distant shore.

XII

Down to that trysting place they fare,
Many people were gathered there—
Father, mother, sister, friend,
    From all the glens, deep-hearted Gael,
Each for some parting brother, blend
    Manhood's tears with woman's wail.
Beneath them on the water's marge,
Lay floating ready the eight-oared barge,
To Achnacarry soon to bear
His clansmen to their young Chief there.
When the Knoydart family reached that crowd,
And heard their lamentations loud,
Behind a green knoll, out of view,
With their young warrior all withdrew—
That knoll which sent, in by-gone days,
Down the long loch the beacon's blaze.
There Angus and his people all
Were waiting them of Rounieval,
And while the old folk, in sorrow peers,
Mingle their common grief and tears,
And Angus, home and parents leaving,
Is set to bear with manly grieving,

Yet one peculiar pang was there,
Which only he and Muriel share—
A pang deep-hid in either breast,
Nor once to alien ear confessed.

XIII

Then Muriel suddenly unbound
  The plaid wherewith herself was drest,
Threw it her brother's shoulders round,
  And wrapt it o'er his manly breast.
"This plaid my own hands dyed and wove,
Memorial of our true home-love;
Let its fast colours symbol be
Of thoughts and prayers that cling to thee."
Then from her breast his mother took
A little Gaelic Bible book—
"For my sake read, and o'er it pray,
We here shall meet when you're far away."
With that, impatient cries wax'd loud—
"Unmoor the barge"—one swift embrace,
  One clinging kiss to each dear face,
And rushing blindly through the crowd,
  Angus and Ronald take their place
Within the boat. The piper blew
The thrilling pibroch of Donald Dhu;
But the sound on the Knoydart weepers fell,
And on many more, like a funeral knell;

And the farther down the loch they sail,
In deeper sadness died the wail,
And their eyes grew dimmer, and yet more dim,
Down the wan water following him—
Watching so fleetly disappear
All that on earth they hold most dear,
Till round the farthest jutting Rhu
The barge, oar-driven, swept from view.
Then from the knoll they turned away,
    And tears no more they cared repress,
But set their face through gloamin' grey,
    Back to the western wilderness.

CANTO SIXTH

THE SOLDIER'S RETURN

I

SEVEN Summers long had fired the glens
  With flush of heather glow;
Seven Winters robed the sheeted Bens
  From head to foot with snow,
And brought their human denizens
  Alternate joy and woe.
When all those years were come and gone,
  One calm October day
The dwellers of Glenmorriston
Forth-looking from their huts at dawn,
Beheld a traveller wandering on
  The long glen west away.
Young he seemed, but travel-worn,
  More weak of gait than youth should be—
A philabeg,[1] but soiled and torn,
Was round him—on his shoulder borne
  A tartan plaid hung carelessly.
"Whence comes yon stranger? whither goes?
  They each to other wondering cry—
" Is he some wanderer from Kintail?

[1] *Philabeg*, Highlander's kilt.

Macdonald's land of Armadale?
  Or Macleod's country, far in Skye?
Or haply some Clanranald man
  From southern market makes his way
Back, where his home by hungry shore
Hears the Atlantic breakers roar
  On Barra and Benbecula."

II

Unasked, unanswering, he passed on,
None spake to him, he spake to none;
But while they questioned whence, and who,
Among themselves, they little knew
  That this was Angus Cameron.
Southward he turned, and noonday found
Him high upon the mountain-ground,
Whence he beheld Glengarry's strath,
With its long winding river path
Streaming beneath him; and discerned
Loch Quoich, amid dark Scours inurned.
And all around it, east and west,
His eye wide-wandering went in quest
Of the old homesteads that he knew,
But the blue smoke from very few
Could he discover; yet he wist
The rest were lost in haze and mist.
So west he turned through mountain doors

That open downward on the shores
Of lone Lochourn.   In that deep pass
　Still lay the little loch, reed-fringed,
With upper marge of greenest grass,
　And birks beyond it, autumn-tinged.
He looked—the summer bothies bare,
All ruinous sank in disrepair;
From them the voice of milking song
And laughter had been absent long.
He paused and listened, but no sound,
　Save of the many rills that come
　Down corrie-beds through the desert dumb;
And over all the voice profound
　Of the great cataract, high aloof,
　Down flashing from the rock-wall roof.

III

The solemn Pass he erst had known
Seemed still as lovely, but more lone,
As westward on with weary pace
He travelled, and no human face
Looked on him, no sound met his ear
That told of man or far or near.
Late had waned the afternoon
　Ere he reached Lochourn's rough shore,
No gleam by random breezes strewn
　Flitted its dark face o'er;

'Neath leaden sky, the waters roll'd
More drear and sullen than of old,
And the silence of all human sounds,
Since he had passed Glengarry bounds,
Lay heavy on his loaded breast
With something of a dim unrest.
But one bright gleam of western day
On the scarr'd forehead of Lurvein lay;
And like an outstretched hand of hope
Seemed beckoning toward yonder cope
Of headland, that projects above
   The sheltered home beside the burn,
Where first he met that young friend's love,
   Who thither will no more return.

IV

But ere he reached the well-known spot,
This way and that he turned in thought—
How 'neath that roof he should declare
The burden of the tale he bare;
How show to those poor hearts forlorn
The frail memorials he had borne
From the far field by Ebro's wave,
Where Ronald fills a soldier's grave;
The plaid, whose every thread was spun
   By Muriel's fingers—the holy book,
Which from his mother's hands the son

Even at their last leave-taking took—
The plaid, which Ronald oft had wound
'Neath cold night-heavens his breast around,
Discoloured, by the grape-shot torn,
In Angus' hands now homeward borne;
That book he oft with reverent heed
By flickering camp-fires woke to read,
That tattered plaid, that treasured book,
   Soiled with his latest life-blood's stains,
On these his loved ones' eyes must look—
   Their all of him that now remains.
Then rose his inward sight before
   Those faces—not as long ago—
But the mother's high brow furrowed o'er
   Deep with the charact'ry of woe,
Which suffering years must have graven there—
And Muriel's cheek, though pale still fair,
Her large blue eyes, thro' weeping dim,
Gazing on these last wrecks of him.

V

But when he reached that headland's crown,
   And stood beside the sole pine-tree,
O'er the sheer precipice gazing down,
   Ah! what a sight was there to see!
Two roofless gables, gaping blank,
   In the damp sea-winds moss-o'ergrown,

And choaked with growth of nettles rank
　　The home-floor, and once warm hearth-stone.
One look sufficed—at once the whole
Sad history flashed upon his soul;
He saw that household's ruined fate,
He knew that all was desolate.
With face to earth he cast him down,
　　As in a stupor long he lay,
And when he woke as from a swoon,
　　And looked abroad, last gleams of day
Even from the highest peaks were gone,
And the lone Loch lay shimmering wan;
From that waste desolated shore
He turned away and looked no more.

VI

From that home, now no more a home,
Up through the dusky pines he clomb;
Up and on, without let or bound,
On-clambering to the high lone ground
Where Knoydart, cloven by sheer defiles,
　　Yawns with torrent-roaring chasms,
Huddled screetan,[1] and rent rock-piles,
　　Nature's work in her wildest spasms:
There, as the darkness deeper fell
And going grew impossible,

　　　　[1] *Screetan*, see p. 31.

Beneath a rock he laid his length,
As one bereft of hope and strength,
And if no further step he passed,
Content that this should be his last.
The hope, that had his heart sustained
    Through years of toil, to ruin hurled—
What shelter any more remained
    In this forsaken world?
What but to share with this poor home
The desolation of its doom?
But they the true, the gentle-hearted,
To what strange bourne had they departed?
Dwell they in noisome city pent?
Or are they tenants now, where rent
None ask, in that drear place of graves,
Which Nevish-Loch at full-tide laves?
Or dwell they far o'er ocean—thrown
Like sea-waifs on some land unknown?

VII

All through that night, I heard him tell,
Strange sounds upon his hearing fell,
Weirdlier sounds than shriek of owl,
Wild cats' scream, hill-foxes' howl,
As though the ancient mountains, rent
To their deep foundations, sent
On the midnight moan on moan,

Ghostly language of their own,
Converse terrible, austere,
Seldom heard by mortal ear.
Then in hurried blinks o' the moon
    Cliff and crag dim-seen appeared
Haggard forms, like eldrich croon,[1]
    Or shapeless beings, vast and weird,
Formless passed before his face
Dwellers of that awesome place.
Angus had been used to bide
    Foeman's shot and shell unmoved—
Badajos—Busaco tried,
    And found his mettle unreproved.
Never before face of man
Had he quailed, but now there ran
Creepings cold thro' all his frame,
O'er his limbs strange trembling came,
And the hair upon his head
Rose erect with very dread
Of this place—this awesome hour,
When the nether world had power.
All he had listened to, as a child,
Of mountain glamourie dark and wild,
To harrow up the soul with fear,
Now palpable to eye and ear,
Seemed gathered to confront him here.

[1] *Eldrich croon*,—Better explained as *croon* for *crone*, unearthly shape, as of an old woman.

VIII

Never stood he so aghast,
Never through such night had passed,
But the dawning came at last :
And when earliest streaks of light
    The eastern peaks had silver-barred,
Behold ! his tarrying place all night
    None other was than Màm-clach-ard.
Forward then, 'mid the glimmer of dawn,
Through the rough Pass he wandered on,
And one by one stars faded on high,
As the tide of light washed up the sky :
But when he reached the eastern door,
Where that high cloven Pass looks o'er
Lochiel's broad mountains, grisly and hoar,
The sun, new-ris'n from the under-world,
    Had all the glens beneath outrolled,
Up the braes the mists had furled,
    And touched their snowy fleeces with gold.
There far below, inlaid between
Steep mountain walls, lay calm and green
Glen Desseray, bright in morning sheen.
As down the rough track Angus trode
The path that led to his old abode,
Calm as of old the lone green glen
Lay stretched before him long miles ten ;

He looked, the braes as erst were fair,
But smoke none rose on the morning air;
He listened, came no blithe cock-crowing
From wakening farms, no cattle-lowing,
No voice of man, no cry of child,
Blent with the loneness of the wild;
Only the wind thro' the bent and ferns,
Only the moan of the corrie-burns.

IX

Can it be? doth this silence tell
   The same sad tale as yester-eve?
My clansmen here who wont to dwell
   Have they too ta'en their last long leave?
Adown this glen too, hath there been
The besom of destruction keen
Sweeping it of its people clean?
That anxious tremour in his breast
One half-hour onward set at rest:
Where once his home had been, now stare
Two gables, roofless, gaunt, and bare;
Two gables, and a broken wall,
Are all now left of Sheniebhal.
The huts around of the old farm-toun,
   Wherein the poorer tenants dwelt,
Moss-covered stone-heaps, crumbling down,
   Into the wilderness slowly melt.

The slopes below, where had gardens been,
Lay thick with rushes darkly green,
The furrows on the braes above
Where erst the flax and the barley throve,
With ferns and heather covered o'er,
To Nature had gone back once more.
And there beneath, the meadow lay,
    The long smooth reach of meadowy ground,
Where intertwining east away
    In loop on loop the river wound :
There, where he heard a former day
The blithe, loud shouting, shinty play,
    Was silence now as the grave profound.
A few steps led to the Mound of the Cave,
A hillock strewn with many a grave,—
Lone place, to which some far and faint
Remembrance of Columban Saint
Come, ages gone, from the Isle of Y,[1]
Gave immemorial sanctity.
There children lost in life's first day
Whom to Kilmallie (that long way),
They did not bear, were laid to sleep,
That o'er them kindred watch might keep,
And mothers thither steal to weep.
There he himself in childhood's morn
Had seen two infants, younger-born,

[1] *Y*, corruptly called *Iona*.

His own sweet brothers, laid to rest ;
And now he came in loving quest
To see their little graves, but they
From sight had melted quite away,—
'Neath touch of time's obscure effacing
   Had passed unto the waste around,
And now no eye could mark the tracing
   'Twixt holy earth, and common ground.

X

Then looking back with one wide ken,
Where stood the Farms, each side the glen—
Tom-na-hua, Cuil, Glach-fern,
Each he clearly could discern ;
Once groups of homes, wherein did dwell
The people he had known so well,
These stood blank skeletons, one and all,
Like his own home, Sheniebhal ;
And he sighed as he gazed on the pathways untrodden,
"These be the homes of the men of Culloden!"
  "This desolation! whence hath come?
What power hath hushed this living glen
Once blithe with happy sounds of men
   Into a wilderness blank and dumb?
Alas for them! leal souls and true!
Kindred and clansmen whom I knew!

Their homes stand roofless on the brae,
And the hearts that loved them, where are they?
Ah me! what days with them I've seen
On the summer braes at the shealings green!
What nights of winter dark and long
Made brief and bright by the joy of song!
The men in peace so gentle and mild,
In battle onset lion-wild,
When the pibroch of Donald Dhu
   Sounded the summons of Lochiel,
From these homes to his standard flew,
   By him stood through woe and weal,
Against Clan-Chattan, age by age
Held his ancient heritage:
And when the Stuart cause was down,
And Lochiel rose for King and Crown,
Who like these same Cameron men
   Gave their gallant heart-blood pure
At Inverlochy, Killiecrankie,
   Preston-pans, Culloden Muir?
And when red vengeance on the Gael
Fell bloody, did their fealty fail?
Did they not screen with lives of men
Their outlawed Prince in desert and den?
And when their Chief fled far away,
Who were his sole support but they?
Alas for them! those faithful men!

And this is all reward they have!
These unroofed homes, this emptied glen
    A forlorn exile, then the grave."

XI

That night, as October winds were tirling [1]
    The birchen woods down Lochiel's long shore,
The wan, dead leaves on the rain-blast whirling,
    A low knock came to our cottage door.
" Lift the latch, bid him welcome," cried my sire.
    Straight a plaided stranger entered in,
And we saw by the light of the red peat fire,
    A long, lank form, and a visage thin.
We children stared—as tho' a ghost
    Had crossed the door—on that face unknown;
But my father cried—" O loved and lost!
    That voice, my brother, is thine own."
Then each on the other's neck they fell,
    And long embraced, and wept aloud;
We children stood—I remember well—
    Our heads in wondering silence bowed.
But when our uncle raised his head,
Gazing around the house, he said—
" I've travelled down Glen Desseray bare,
    Looked on our desolate home to-day,
But those my heart most longed for, where?

[1] *Tirling*, slightly touching, thrilling.

Father and mother, where are they?
For them has their own country found
No home, save underneath the ground?"
  "Too truly has your heart divined,"
My father answered him, "for they
Came hither but not long to stay—
With the fall o' the year away they dwined,
Not loth another home to find,
  Where none could say them nay.
Above their heads to-night the sward
Is green in Kilmallie's old kirkyard."

XII

In vain for him the board we strewed,
He little cared for rest or food—
On this alone intent—to know,
Whence had come the ruin and woe.
"Tell me, O tell me whence," he cried,
"Hath spread this desolation wide;
What ministers of dark despair—
From nether pit or upper air—
On the poor country of the Gael,
Have breathed this blasting blight and bale.
By lone Lochourn, too, I have been,
And Runieval in ruin seen;
I know that home is desolate—
Tell me the dwellers' earthly fate."

"Ah, these are gone, with many more,"
My father said, "to a far-off shore,
By some great lake, whereof we know
Only the name—Ontario.
They tell us there are broad lands there,
Whereof whoever will may share,
Great forests—trees of giant stem—
Glen-mallie pines are naught to them.
But of all that we nothing know,
Save the great name, Ontario."
"But whence came all this ruin? Tell
From whom the cruel outrage fell,
On our poor people." With a sigh
My father fain had put him by;
"A tale so full of sorrow and wrong,
To-night to tell were all too long,
Weary and hungry thou need'st must be—
Sit down at the board we have spread for thee!"
I wot we had spread it of our best.
But for him our dainties had little zest;
Nor would he eat or drink, until
Of that dark tale he had heard his fill.

XIII

Not many days my father's roof
   That soldier-brother could retain;
To wander to far lands aloof

His heart was on the strain.
But while within our home he stayed,
   He turned him every day,
To where, in sombre beech-trees' shade
His parents both are lowly laid,
   'Neath mountain flag-stone grey.
The last time that he lingered there,
   Some moss he gathered from the grave,
The one memorial he could bear,
Where'er his wandering feet might fare,
   Beyond the western wave.
And then he left my father's door,
And bidding farewell evermore
To dwellers on this mountain shore,
He set his face to that world afar,
On which descends the evening star.
We never knew what there befell—
Some said that he found Muriel,
With her old parents yet alive,
Where still Glengarry clansmen thrive,
And there, on great Ontario's side,
He led her home, his wedded bride.
But others whispered 'twas not so—
That ere he came her head was low,
And nothing left him but to keep,
Far in primeval forest deep,
Watch o'er his loved one's lonely sleep,

And her poor parents' age to tend,
Till they should to the grave descend.
Authentic voice none o'er the sea
Came, telling how these things might be—
His fate in that far land was dumb,
And silent as the world to come.
We only know such fervent thought
Of all the past within him wrought,
That, ere he sailed, he turned aside,
That dreary moor to wander o'er,
Where the last gleam of Albyn's pride
In blood went down to rise no more;
And while the bark on Moray Firth,
That bore him from his native earth,
Waited the breeze to fill her sail,
This coronach, this woful wail,
He breathed for the down-trodden Gael.

1

The moorland wide, and waste, and brown,
Heaves far and near, and up and down—
Few trenches green the desert crown,
    And these are the graves of Culloden!

2

What mournful thoughts to me they yield,
Gazing with sorrow yet unhealed,
On Scotland's last and saddest field—
    O! the desolate Moor of Culloden!

3

Ah me! what carnage vain was there!
What reckless fury—mad despair!
On this wide moor such odds to dare—
 O, the wasted lives of Culloden!

4

For them laid there, the brave and young,
How many a mother's heart was wrung!
How many a coronach sad was sung,
 O, the green, green graves of Culloden!

5

What boots it now to point and tell,
Here the Clan Chattan bore them well,
Shame-maddened, yonder Keppoch fell—
 Lavish of life on Culloden.

6

Here Camerons clove the red line through,
There Stuarts dared what men could do,
Charged lads of Athole, staunch and true,
 To the cannon mouths on Culloden.

7

In vain the wild onset—in vain
Claymores cleft English skulls in twain—

The cannon fire poured in like rain,
    Mowing down the clans on Culloden.

8

Through all the glens, from shore to shore,
What wailing went! but that is o'er—
Hearts now are cold, that once were sore,
    For the loved ones lost on Culloden.

9

—The Highlands all one hunting ground,
Where men are few, and deer abound,
And desolation broods profound
    O'er the homes of the men of Culloden.

10

That, too, will pass—the hunter's deer,
The drover's sheep will disappear,
But when another race will you rear,
    Like the men that died at Culloden?

THE MOUNTAIN WALK[1]

PART I

FROM beaten paths and common tasks reprieved,
   My face I set towards the lonely grounds
Where Moidart and Lochaber, northward heaved,
   Meet with rough Knoydart bounds.

And with me went an aged man on whom
   Still lightly hung his threescore years and ten,
Intent to see once more before the tomb
   His long-unpeopled glen.

O'er "Faeth,"[2] "Maam," "Gual," each shape of mountain-pass,
   From morn to eve, an autumn day we clomb
A lone waste wilderness where no man was,
   Nor any human home;

And looked o'er mountain backs, misty or bared,
   Ridged multitudinous to the northern bourn,

---

[1] See Note at end.
[2] In Gaelic *Feìth*, sluggish pool in marshy moorland; *Màm*, high rounded hill; *Guala*, high ridge, literally *shoulder*.

Where high o'er all the great scours¹ watch and guard
    Loch Nevish and Lochourn ;

Saw far to west through yawning gaps upleap
    Dark Moidart mountains with their clov'n defiles,
And here and there let in the great blue deep,
    With the far outer Isles ;

While close beneath our feet clear streams were flowing
    Down long glens walled the steep dark hills between,
With their long streaks of grassy margin glowing
    Bright with resplendent sheen.

And by the stream's grass-mounds and grey-mossed heaps
    Lay, once the homes where thriving men had been,
And far up corries,² where the white burn leaps,
    Were pleasant airidhs³ green.

But no smoke rose from any old abode ;
    From the green summer shealings came no song,
No face of man looked on us where we trode,
    From dawn to gloamin' long.

Only high up hoarse-barking raven's croak
    Knelled on the iron crags, or glead's wild screams,

---

[1] *Scours*, here used for rocky frowning heights.
[2] *Corries*, hillside hollows.   [3] *Airidhs*, shealing-pastures.

And down the awful precipices broke
    The everlasting streams;

The while the old man told how times remote
   Had named the balloch [1] from some famous man,
Slain in old battle when the Camerons smote
    Their foes of Chattan clan;

Or on "the squally shoulder" he would pause,
   And, pointing to grey stones, would whisper, "Here
The mourners builded Evan's cairn, because
    They rested with his bier

"On the long journey from his native glen,
   Down to his last home by the sea-loch side;"
And, "There by night and weariness o'erta'en,
    Long since a shepherd died."

And then more lightly, "O'er these very knowes [2]
   I ran the browse [3] upon my wedding-day
With other lads to win my young bride's house,
    Now fifty years away."

Late in the afternoon my steps he stayed
   On a high mountain pass, and bade me look,
Where the burn, plunging from the height, had made
    One small and sheltered nook:

---

[1] *Balloch*, narrow pass.   [2] *Knowes*, knolls.
[3] *Browse*, horse race run sometimes at country weddings.

"Beneath that bank we rested us at eve,
  The first day's weary journey ended, when
Full sixty years since we were forced to leave
  For ever our dear glen.

"A day it was of lamentation sore,
  As we set face against the steep ascent,
Slowly the lowing cattle moved before,
  Behind we weeping went.

"And well we might; the old folk from that day
  Found never home like that they had resigned;
And we—thenceforth our happy childhood lay
  In that far glen behind."

And so with talk like this the day wore on,
  No rock unnamed, no cairn without its tale,
Till, from the western scours[1] the last gleams gone,
  To the deep-shadowed vale

Down through Leaëna-vaata slow we passed,
  "The hollow of the wolf," so named of old,
Since hunters there o'ertook and slew the last
  Grim spoiler of the fold.

There where Loch Aragat hath his utmost bound
  And from the western glens the waters meet,
Beneath the kindly shepherd's roof we found
  Welcome, and warm retreat.

[1] *Scours*, here used for mountain-tops.

PART II

All night enfolded in the lap of Bens,[1]
  Around our sleep the loud and lulling sound
Of many waters meeting from the glens
  Made lullaby profound.

Next day the westering morn our guide we make,
  Where a strong stream in jambs of granite pent,
From pool to pool, down-plunging to the lake,
  Hath grooved itself a vent.

That strait throat passed, back falls the mountain's bound,
  Before us there out-spread in silence, lay,
With loop on loop of river interwound,
  Long, green Glen Desseray.

A long, flat, meadowy, strath of natural grass,
  Where calm, from side to side, the river flows,
After the turmoil of yon splintered pass,
  Loitering in slow repose.

Each side steep mountain-flanks wall the green flat,
  To west the long glen closes, grimly barred
By the stern-precipiced shelves of Scour-na-naat
  And by dark Maam-clach-ard.

[1] *Ben*, mountain-head; by metaphor used for the mountain itself.

THE MOUNTAIN WALK

There as we stood on the mute glen to gaze
    The old man pointed to the hillocks green,
Where, either side the strath, in former days,
    The Clansmen's homes had been;

Homes that had reared the Camerons, who in old
    Centuries of ceaseless battle, true and leal,
Against Clan Chattan had been brave to hold
    His country for Lochiel;

Who, in the latest rising of the clans,
    For King and Chief, devoted hearts and pure,
Had led the crashing charge at Preston-pans,
    Died on Culloden moor.

For all those homesteads only here and there
    A gaunt, grey, weathered gable—for the hum
Of many human voices, on the air
    Blank, aweful silence dumb.

Only the hill-burns down the corries broke,
    Only one hern harsh-screaming from the fen,
And but one shepherd's solitary smoke,
    Far in the upper glen.

Then, one by one, the old man, sad at heart,
    Pointed the stances,[1] where in childhood time
From four blithe farm-towns, each a mile apart,
    He had seen the blue smoke climb.

[1] *Stances*, sites.

THE MOUNTAIN WALK

Two on the north side, dry on ferny knowes,
    The noonday sun had welcomed with frank look,
The southern two, withdrawn 'neath high-hill brows,
    Each cower'd in bielded[1] nook.

Then closer drawing 'neath rank weeds he showed
    The larachs[2] of the homes, wall, hearth and floor,
Where in each town large brotherhoods abode,
    Twelve families and more.

And as he traced each home, the names he told
    Of men and women who there once had been,
How lived and died they in wild days of old,
    What weirdly sights had seen.

And last he led me to his own farm-town,
    Even to his father's home—there lay the hearth
Grey-lichened, walls around it crumbled down,
    Till all but blent with earth.

"There yawned the window to the crag behind,
    Through which my grandsire gallant burst away,
When two red-coats, who had him in the wind,
    After Culloden day,

"The threshold crossed to seize him; fleet of foot,
    He took the crag—they fired and missed their aim,

---

[1] *Bielded*, sheltered.   [2] *Larachs*, foundations.

Then, throwing down their guns, in hot pursuit,
    Fast on his track they came.

"He slacked his speed, and let the foremost near,
    Then heaved a slag[1] of rock, and laid him low;
The chase was over—he left free from fear,
    Forth to the hills to go."

And then, with lowered voice and deepened feeling,
    Pointing one spot upon the floor, he said,
"Here on these very stones we bairns were kneeling,
    And there my father prayed,

"One stormy Sabbath-night, when wild winds hurried
    A loosened snow-heap from the crag, and o'er
The rigging[2] rolled it clean, and deeply buried
    The house, and blocked the door

"With a great boulder." These and many more
    Tales through the glen beguiled us west away
O'er Maam-clach-ard to dark Loch Nevish's shore
    Down with declining day.

There, 'neath a roof, where people of the old kind
    Still keep the ancient faith, through the deep calm,
All night we heard the cataracts behind
    Down-thundering from the Maam;

---

[1] *Slag*, loose fragment.   [2] *Rigging*, roof.

The while they told how oft when no wind stirred,
    Unearthly sounds the mountain stillness rent
At midnight, by belated travellers heard,
    As through the Maam they went;

And apparitions when the spirit fled,
    Crossing the gaze of melancholy seers,
And trystings where the living met the dead
    By lonely mountain meres;

All the weird, visionary lore that lives
    Still by the dim lochs of the western sea,
And to that region and its people gives
    Strange eerie glamourie.

Next morn we clomb the Maam with eastward foot
    And walked the higher ranges of the glen,
Looked on green summer shealings, long left mute
    By old Glen-Desseray men.

One last look back—there lay the glen inlaid
    Deep in its walling hills—a meadowy strath,
Through which in loop on loop the river strayed,
    A slowly-winding path.

And all the west, jagg'd precipices riven
    With gorge and gully and ravine black-gloomed,
Closed in—above them in the twilight heaven
    The great peaks ghostly loomed.

THE MOUNTAIN WALK

All these days, as we wandered, morn to eve,
    The old man, piece by piece, the tale unrolled,
How once the Cameron clansmen wont to live
    Within these glens of old.

Things too his grandsire and his sire had seen,
    After Culloden, till the ruthless time
That swept the glens of all their people clean,
    Things mute in prose or rhyme.

Written before 1870.

A DREAM OF GLEN-SALLACH [1]

THAT summer glen is far away,
  Who loved me then, their graves are green,
But still that dell and distant day,
  Lie bright in memory's softest sheen.

Are these still there, outspread in space,
  The grey mossed-trees, the mountain stream?
Or in some ante-natal place,
  That only cometh back in dream?

There first upon my soul was cast
  Dim reverence, blent with glorious thrills,
From out an old heroic past,
  Lapped in the older calm of hills.

Still after thirty summers loom
  On dreaming hours the lichened trees,
The ivied walls, the warrior's tomb,
  'Mid those old mountain sanctities.

How awed I stood! where once had kneeled
  The pilgrims by the holy well,

[1] See Note at end.

O'er which, through centuries unrepealed,
   Rome's consecration still doth dwell.

How crept among the broken piles!
   And clansmen's grave-stones moss-o'ergrown,
Where rests the Lord of all the Isles,
   With plaid and claymore graven in stone.

In deep of noon, mysterious dread
   Fell on me in that glimmering glen,
Till, as from haunted ground, I fled
   Back to the kindly homes of men.

Thanks to that glen! its scenery blends
   With childhood's most ideal hour,
When Highland hills I made my friends,
   First owned their beauty, felt their power.

Still, doubtless, o'er Kilbrannan Sound,
   As lovely lights from Arran gleam,
'Mid hills that gird Glen-Sallach round,
   As happy children dream their dream.

The western sea, as deep of tone,
   Is murmuring 'gainst that caverned shore;
But, one whole generation gone,
   No more those haunts are ours, no more.

This poem, and the six following, were published in 1864.

THE MOOR OF RANNOCH

O'ER the dreary moor of Rannoch
   Calm these hours of Sabbath shine;
But no kirk-bell here divideth
   Week-day toil from rest divine.

Ages pass, but save the tempest,
   Nothing here makes toil or haste;
Busy weeks nor restful Sabbath
   Visit this abandoned waste.

Long ere prow of earliest savage
   Grated on blank Albyn's shore,
Lay these drifts of granite boulders,
   Weather-bleached and lichened o'er.

Beuchaille Etive's furrowed visage,
   To Schihallion looked sublime,
O'er a wide and wasted desert,
   Old and unreclaimed as time.

THE MOOR OF RANNOCH

Yea! a desert wide and wasted,
    Washed by rain-floods to the bones;
League on league of heather blasted,
    Storm-gashed moss, grey boulder-stones;

And along these dreary levels,
    As by some stern destiny placed,
Yon sad lochs of black moss water
    Grimly gleaming on the waste;

East and west, and northward sweeping,
    Limitless the mountain plain,
Like a vast low heaving ocean,
    Girdled by its mountain chain:

Plain, o'er which the kingliest eagle,
    Ever screamed by dark Lochowe,
Fain would droop a laggard pinion,
    Ere he touched Ben-Aulder's brow:

Mountain-girdled,—there Bendoran
    To Schihallion calls aloud,
Beckons he to lone Ben-Aulder,
    He to Nevis crowned with cloud.

Cradled here old Highland rivers,
    Etive, Cona, regal Tay,
Like the shout of clans to battle,
    Down the gorges break away.

And the Atlantic sends his pipers
    Up yon thunder-throated glen,
O'er the moor at midnight sounding
    Pibrochs never heard by men.

Clouds, and mists, and rains before them
    Crowding to the wild wind tune,
Here to wage their all-night battle,
    Unbeheld by star and moon.

Loud the while down all his hollows,
    Flashing with a hundred streams,
Corrie-bah from out the darkness
    To the desert roars and gleams.

Sterner still, more drearly driven,
    There o' nights the north wind raves,
His long homeless lamentation,
    As from Arctic seamen's graves.

Till his mighty snow-sieve shaken
    Down hath blinded all the lift,[1]
Hid the mountains, plunged the moorland
    Fathom-deep in mounded drift.

Such a time, while yells of slaughter
    Burst at midnight on Glencoe,
Hither flying babes and mothers
    Perished 'mid the waste of snow.

[1] *Lift*, sky.

Countless storms have scrawled unheeded
   Characters o'er these houseless moors ;
But that night engraven forever
   In all human hearts endures.

Yet the heaven denies not healing
   To the darkest human things,
And to-day some kindlier feeling
   Sunshine o'er the desert flings.

Though the long deer-grass is moveless,
   And the corrie-burns[1] are dry ;
Music comes in gleams and shadows
   Woven beneath the dreaming eye.

Desert not deserted wholly !
   Where such calms as these can come,—
Never tempest more majestic
   Than this boundless silence dumb.

---

[1] *Corrie-burn*, stream in hollow on hillside.

THE LASS OF LOCH LINNE

THE spray may drive, the rain may pour,
    Knee-deep in brine, what careth she?
Her brother's boat she'll drag to shore,
    Aloud she'll sing her Highland glee.

Her feet and head alike all bare,
    A drenched plaid swathed about her form,
Around her floats the Highland air,
    Within the Highland blood beats warm.

All night they've toiled and not in vain :
    To count and store the fish be thine ;
Then drench thy clothes in morning rain,
    And dry them in the noon sunshine !

The gleam breaks through, the day will clear,
    Then to the peats up yonder glen ;
O there is life and freedom here !
    That cannot breathe 'mid throngs of men.

What has thy life and history been?
    Brave lass upon this wind-beat shore!
I may not guess—at distance seen,
    A nameless image, and no more.

Sweet chime the sea beside thy home,
    Thy fire blink bright on heartsome meal!
No more of dearth or clearance come
    To darken down thine own Lochiel!

THE FOREST OF SLI'-GAOIL

THAT IS, THE HILL OF LOVE [1]

IN this bare treeless forest lone,
By winds Atlantic overblown,
I sit and hear the weird wind pass
Drearily through the long bent-grass;
And think how that low sighing heard
By Ossian, when no wind was stirred,
Filled his old sightless eyes with tears,
His soul with thoughts of other years,
For the spirits of the men he mourned
In that low eerie sound returned.

And doth not this bleak forest ground
Live in old epic song renowned?
Of him the chief who came of yore
To hunting of the mighty boar,
And left the deed, to float along
The dateless stream of Highland song,
A maid's lorn love, a chief's death-toil,
Still speaking in thy name, Sli'-gaoil!

[1] See Note at end.

Well now may harp of Ossian moan,
Through long bent-grass and worn grey stone :
But how could song so long ago,
Come loaded with still elder wo ?
Were then, as now, these hills o'ercast
With shadows of some long-gone past ?
Did winds, that wandered o'er them, chíme
Melodies of a lorn foretime ?
As now, the very mountain burns
For something sigh that not returns ?

RETURN TO NATURE

On the braes[1] around Glenfinnan
Fast the human homes are thinning,
And the wilderness is winning
   To itself these graves again.
Names or dates here no man knoweth,
O'er grey headstones heather groweth,
Up Loch-Shiel the sea-wind bloweth
   Over sleep of nameless men.

Who were those forgotten sleepers?
Herdsmen strong, fleet forest-keepers,
Aged men, or widowed weepers
   For their foray-fallen ones?
Babes cut off 'mid childhood's prattle,
Men who lived with herds and cattle,
Clansmen from Culloden battle,
   Camerons, or Clandonald's sons?

Blow ye winds, and rains effacing!
Blur the words of love's fond tracing!

[1] *Braes*, hillsides.

Nature to herself embracing
    All that human hearts would keep :
What they knew of good or evil
Faded, like the dim primeval
Day that saw the vast upheaval
    Of these hills that hold their sleep.

CAILLEACH BEIN-Y-VREICH [1]

WEIRD wife of Bein-y-Vreich! horo! horo!
    Aloft in the mist she dwells;
Vreich horo! Vreich horo! Vreich horo!
    All alone by the lofty wells.

Weird, weird wife! with the long grey locks,
    She follows her fleet-foot stags,
Noisily moving through splintered rocks,
    And crashing the grisly crags.

Tall wife! with the long grey hose, in haste
    The rough stony beach she walks;
But dulse [2] or seaweed she will not taste,
    Nor yet the green kail stalks.

And I will not let my herds of deer,
    My bonny red deer go down;
I will not let them down to the shore,
    To feed on the sea-shells brown.

O better they love in the corrie's recess,
    Or on mountain top to dwell,

---

[1] See Note at end.   [2] *Dulse*, sea-celery.

And feed by my side on the green green cress,
    That grows by the lofty well.

Broad Bein-y-Vreich is grisly and drear,
    But wherever my feet have been,
The well-springs start for my darling deer,
    And the grass grows tender and green.

And there high up on the calm nights clear,
    Beside the lofty spring,
They come to my call, and I milk them there,
    And a weird wild song I sing.

But when hunter men round my dun deer prowl,
    I will not let them nigh;
Through the rended cloud I cast one scowl,
    They faint on the heath and die.

And when the north wind o'er the desert bare
    Drives loud, to the corries below
I drive my herds down, and bield [1] them there
    From the drifts of the blinding snow.

Then I mount the blast, and we ride full fast,
    And laugh as we stride the storm,
I, and the witch of the Cruachan Ben,
    And the scowling-eyed Seul-Gorm.

[1] *Bield*, shelter.

DESOLATION

By the wee birchen corries lie patches of green,
Where gardens and bareheaded bairnies have been,
But the huts now are rickles [1] of stones nettle-grown,
And the once human homes, e'en their names are unknown.

But the names that this side the Atlantic have perished,
'Mid far western forests still dearly are cherished,
There men talk of each spot, on the hills that surround
Their long vanished dwellings, as paradise ground.

Not a pass in these hills, not a cairn, nor a corrie,
But lives by the log-fire in legend and story;
And darkly the cloud on their countenance gathers,
As they think on those desolate homes of their fathers.

O hearts, to the hills of old memory true!
In the land of your love there are mourners for you,

[1] *Rickles*, heaps.

As they wander by peopleless lochside and glen,
Where the red deer are feeding o'er homesteads of men.

For the stillness they feel o'er the wilderness spread
Is not nature's own silence, but that of the dead;
E'en the lone piping plover, and small corrie burn
Seem sighing for those that will never return.

A CRY FROM CRAIG-ELLACHIE

COMPOSED AFTER TRAVELLING TO INVERNESS FOR THE FIRST TIME IN THE NEWLY-OPENED HIGHLAND RAILWAY, 1864

I

LAND of bens and glens and corries,
Headlong rivers, ocean floods!
Have we lived to see this outrage
On your haughty solitudes?

Yea! there burst invaders stronger
On the mountain-barriered land,
Than the Ironsides of Cromwell,
Or the bloody Cumberland.

Spanning Tay, and curbing Tummel,
Hewing with rude mattocks down
Killiecrankie's birchen chasm;
What reck they of old renown?

Cherished names! how disenchanted!
Hark the railway porter roar,—

"Ho! Blair Athole! Dalna-spidal!
Ho! Dalwhinnie! Aviemore!"

Garry, cribbed with mound and rampart,
Up his chafing bed we sweep;
Scare from his lone lochan[1]-cradle
The charmed immemorial sleep.

Grisly, storm-resounding Badenoch,
With grey boulders scattered o'er,
And cairns of forgotten battles,
Is a wilderness no more.

Ha! we start the ancient stillness,
Swinging down the long incline,
Over Spey, by Rothiemurchus'
Forests of primeval pine.

"Boar of Badenoch," "Sow of Athole,"[2]
Hill by hill behind me cast,
Rock and craig and moorland reeling,
Scarce Craig-Ellachie stands fast.[3]

Dark Glen More and cloven Glen Feschie,
Loud along these desolate tracts

[1] *Lochan*, small lake.
[2] Two neighbouring mountains, thus named.
[3] "Stand fast, Craig-Ellachie," is the war-cry of the Clan Grant.

Hear the shrieking whistle louder
Than their headlong cataracts.

On, still on—let drear Culloden
For clan-slogans [1] hear the scream—
Shake, ye woods by Beauly river,
Start, thou beauty-haunted Dhruim.

Northward still the iron horses!
Naught may stay their destined path
Till they snort by Pentland surges,
Stun the cliffs of far Cape Wrath.

II

Must then pass, quite disappearing
From their glens, the ancient Gael?
In and in must Saxon wriggle,
Southern, cockney, more prevail?

Clans long gone, and pibrochs going,
Shall the patriarchal tongue
From the mountains fade for ever
With its names and memories hung?

Ah! you say, it little recketh;
Let the ancient manners go:

[1] *Clan-slogan*, war-cry.

Heaven will work, through their destroying,
Some end greater than you know.

Be it so, but will Invention,
With her smooth mechanic arts,
Bid arise the old Highland warriors,
Beat again warm Highland hearts?

Nay! whate'er of good they herald,
Whereso' comes that hideous roar,
The old charm is disenchanted,
The old Highlands are no more.

III

Yet, I know there lie all lonely,
Still to feed thought's loftiest mood,
Countless glens undesecrated,
Many an awful solitude.

Many a burn, in unknown corries
Down dark rocks the white foam flings,
Fringed with ruddy berried rowans,
Fed from everlasting springs.

Still there sleep unnumbered lochans
Far away 'mid deserts dumb,
Where no human roar yet travels,
Never tourist's foot hath come.

Many a scour,[1] like bald sea-eagle,
Scalped all white with boulder piles,
Stands against the sunset, eyeing
Ocean and the outmost Isles.

If e'en these should fail, I'll get me
To some rock roared round by seas:
There to drink calm Nature's freedom
Till they bridge the Hebrides.

[1] *Scour*, rocky prominent height.

BEN CRUACHAN

1

ONCE more by mighty Cruachan, and once more
   Across fair isleted Lochowe,
I gaze upon the wood-fringed precipiced shore,
Up the broad girth of green, the gorges hoar,
   To that majestic brow.

2

Between Lochowe and Etive how that pile
   Fills all the interspace! and bars
With his great feet yon river-girt defile,
His lonely forehead communing the while
   With cloud and sun and stars.

3

And then thy wealth of waters—here they creep,
   Lapping thy feet with tender lave;
Yon salt sea-tides around thy basement sweep,
While midway down from crags great cataracts leap,
   Blowing their trumpets brave.

4

And yet beneath these splintered pinnacles,
   Soaring in strength and majesty,
Down that broad bosom what bright greenness dwells:
The like on Scotland's Bens or English Fells
   No otherwhere you see.

5

O ! I could lie and gaze—forever gaze—
   While, in the movement and the sway
Of sun and shadow o'er these broad green braes,
Hour after hour the bright autumnal days
   Are dreaming themselves away !

6

And thou dost seem a being self-enwrapt
   In thine own thought, great Cruachan !
Whether in storm enveloped and storm-capt,
Or in pure light from base to summit lapt,
   Taking no note of man.

7

Yet sure some buried histories thou hast
   Of Scotland's old heroic men ;
Have not their stalwart strides along thee past,
Have not thy corries to their bugle blast
   Startled, O Cruachan Ben ?

8

O for some ancient bard this day to come,
  Some grey Glenorchy chronicler,
And name each rock, pass, mountain track; and some
Of the mute histories here lying dumb
  From long oblivion stir.

9

How when the wild kerne [1] came from Erin, borne
  At Edward's hest, the land to win,
Wight Wallace left his Stirling rock at morn,
And ere night fell, at yonder pass of Lorn
  Had shut the caitiff in.

10

There yawns the gap on Benavourie's slope
  Through which Sir Neil, with morning light
Appearing, closed the flying chief from hope,
And by yon track that grooves the mountain-slope—
  Still called the path of flight—

11

Down that dark pass through which the river raves
  Drave him in rout and all his men :—
Beyond the stream, in Craiganuni's caves
They sought a shelter, and they found their graves
  Under the o'ershadowing Ben.

[1] See Note at end.

12

Anon he'd tell how Bruce in war array,
   Secure of Scotland and her Crown,
Marched to this same pass, thirsting to repay
The despite Lorn had done him on the day
   When fortune held him down ;

13

And how Lorn met him in yon narrow halse,[1]
   And barred the way with targe and spear,
Till gude Sir James, rounding the Corrieglass,[2]
From yonder crag came thundering down the pass,
   And smote him, flank and rear.

14

Ah me ! as through the gorge the battle boiled,
   What wild shrieks there went up to heaven
As forward Bruce through rocks and brushwood toiled,
And backward Lorn with all his host recoiled
   To death and ruin driven.

15

About thee many a slogan more hath knelled !
   Thou sawest how many a bloody crime
When up thy corries Campbell bloodhounds yelled,
Hunting Clan Alpine from the glens they held
   From immemorial time.

---

[1] *Halse*, throat of a glen.   [2] *Corrieglass*, grey hollow.

16

All these into thy silent self thou hast
   Absorbed, and gentler things than these;
The loving looks Poets have on thee cast,—
Wordsworth and Walter Scott, what time they past
   With their high melodies.

17

And year by year have come hearts old and young,
   Native and stranger too, to shed on thee
Affection not less deep, albeit unsung,
Till with an air thou seemest overhung
   Of mute humanity.

18

There till the human story shall fulfil
   Itself, O Cruachan, thou shalt stay.
—Then shall it be by strong convulsive thrill
That thou shalt pass, or slow mutations still
   Preluding that blest day

19

To which the toiling ages labour on
   When, all the contradiction healed,
All the long travail of the creature done,
He, looked-for long, shall come, the Righteous One
   To heart and eye revealed?

Written August 1869.

ON VISITING DRUIM-A LIATH

The Birthplace of Duncan Ban Macintyre [1]

The homes long are gone, but enchantment still lingers
  These green knolls around, where thy young life began,
Sweetest and last of the old Celtic singers,
  Bard of the Monadh-dhu, blithe Donach Ban!

Never 'mid scenes of earth fairer or grander
  Poet first lifted his eyelids on light,
Free through these glens, o'er these mountains to wander,
  And make them his own by the true minstrel right.

Around thee the meeting and green interlacing
  Of clear-flowing waters and far-winding glens,
Lovely inlaid in the mighty embracing
  Of sombre pine forests and storm-riven Bens:

[1] See Note at end.

Behind thee, these crowding Peaks, region of mystery,
   Fed thy young spirit with broodings sublime;
Grey cairn and green hillock, each breathing some
      history
   Of the weird under-world, or the wild battle-time.

Thine were Ben-Starrav, Stop-gyre, Meal-na-ruadh,
   Mantled in storm-gloom, or bathed in sunshine;
Streams from Cor-oran, Glashgower, and Glen-fuadh
   Made music for thee, where their waters combine.

But over all others, thy darling Ben Doran
   Held thee entranced with his beautiful form,
With looks ever-changing thy young fancy storing,
   Gladness of sunshine, and terror of storm,—

Opened to thee his most secret recesses,
   Taught thee the lore of the red-deer and roe,
Showed thee them feed on the green mountain cresses,
   Drink the cold wells above lone Doirè-chro.

There thine eye watched them go up the hill-passes,
   At sunrise rejoicing, a proud jaunty throng;
Learnt the herbs that they love, the small flow'rs
      and hill grasses,
   To make these for ever bloom green in thy song.

Yet, child of the wilderness! nursling of nature!
  Would the hills e'er have taught thee the true
    minstrel art,
Had not a visage, more lovely of feature,
  The fountain unsealed of thy tenderer heart?

The maiden that dwelt by the side of Maam-haarie,
  Seen from thy home-door—a vision of joy—
Morning and even, the young fair-haired Mary
  Moving about at her household employ.

High on Bendoa, and stately Benchallader,
  Leaving the dun deer in safety to hide,
Fondly thy doating eye dwelt on her, followed her,
  Tenderly wooed her, and won her thy bride.

O! well for the maiden who found such a lover!
  And well for the Poet; to whom Mary gave
Her fulness of heart, until, life's journey over,
  She lay down beside him to rest in the grave.

From the bards of to-day, and their sad songs that
    darken
  The sunshine with doubt, wring the bosom with
    pain,
How gladly we fly to the shealings, and hearken
  The clear mountain gladness that sounds through
    thy strain!

In the uplands with thee is no doubt or misgiving,
    But strength, joy, and freedom Atlantic winds blow,
And kind thoughts are there, and the pure simple living
    Of the warm-hearted Gael in the glens long ago.

The muse of old Maro hath pathos and splendour,
    The long lines of Homer in majesty roll;
But to me Donach Ban breathes a feeling more tender,
    More akin to the child-heart that sleeps in my soul.

Written September 1869.

SCHIHALLION

I WATCHED the sun fall down with prone descent
Sheer on Schihallion's spear-like pinnacle,
Which, as he touched it, cleaved his solid orb
As a great warrior's spear might split the rim
Of a broad foeman's shield; A moment more,
The liquid fire, ere to the centre cleft,
Had re-assumed his own supremacy,
And fused the granite peak into the mass
Of his own molten glory.   Anon he rolled
Off from the spear-like peak majestically,
Along the sharp-edged shoulder north away,
Rolling, and sinking slow till he became
A bright belt, then an eye of light, then dipped
Down to the under-world, and all was gone.
Then all the mountain's eastern precipice,
Though dark in purple shadow, loomed out large;
As proud to have absorbed one sunset more,
And conscious of its own stability.
A solemn pause it was, an awful thrill

Of silence audible, as though the tide
Of time were meeting with eternity :—
Such is the awful hush, the prayer-like pause,
When some good life benign has passed in peace
From earth, and mourners feel that all is well.

Written August 6, 1870.

TORRIDON GLEN[1]

Oh marvellous Glen of Torridon,
   With thy flanks of granite wall,
And noon-silence more than midnight grim
   To overawe and appal!

Many a year I have wandered
   A thousand corries and glens,
But never a one so awesome as thou,
   'Mid thy grimness and terror of Bens.

Benyea, magnificent Alp,
   Blanched bare, and bald, and white,
His forehead, like old sea eagle's scalp,
   Seen athwart the sunset light!

Liaguch, rising sheer
   From river-bed up to the sky,
Grey courses of masonry, tier on tier,
   And pinnacles splintered on high!

[1] See Note at end.

Splintered, contorted, and riven
  As though, from the topmost crown
Some giant plougher his share had driven
  In a hundred furrows sheer down.

On the further flank of the glen,
  Sweeping in wonderous line,
Scourdhu, Benlia, Bendamh
  Their weirdly forms combine.

At every turn new grouped,
  Fantastic features and forms,
Cataract-cloven and corrie-scooped ;
  Homes of the thunder storms.

Mysterious Glen Torridon,
  What marvels, night and day
Light, mist, and cloud will be working here
  When we are far away !

When the young dawn makes its home
  On Liaguch's wrinkled brow,
Or the moonlight moves o'er yon cataract's foam,
  What painter can work as thou ?

Through these Peaks when the thunder is rolled,
It were worth all the poems of men

To hear the discourse these Brethren hold
    As they shout over Torridon Glen.

When the great Atlantic winds
    Come blowing with rack and rain,
From its caves and crannies the glen unbinds
    The peal of how grand a refrain!

And then, when the storms are o'er,
    The relapse to the solemn sleep—
The mountain sabbath that ever more
    A sanctuary here doth keep!

With silence, sound, light and mist,
    Labouring or lying still,
Painter or Poet, or whate'er thou list,
    What, compared with thine, their skill

To lift or o'erawe the heart?
    —The power that dwells in thee,
Simple, sublime, and strong as thou art,
    Is of Eternity.

The world weak with sin hath grown,
    The nations are smit with decay;
The order of things Earth long hath known
    Must pass with a crash away.

Only two things shall stand
Healthful and undecayed—
The will of God, and this mountain land,
Which He, not man, hath made.

Written July 28, 29, 1871.

LOCH TORRIDON [1]

I

CHILD of the far-off ocean flood!
What wayward mood hath made thee fain
To leave thy wide Atlantic main
For this hill-girdled solitude?
To wind away through kyles and creeks,
Past island, cliff, and promontory,
And lose thyself 'mid grisly peaks
And precipices scarred and hoary?
Can it be thou weariest
Of ocean's turbulence and unrest,
Of driving wind and weltering foam,
And, longing for some peaceful home,
Dost hither come in hope to reap
Thy portion of the mountain sleep,
That underneath all changes broods
In these eternal solitudes?
And, far away from plash and roar
Of breaking billows, evermore

[1] See Note at end.

Inlapt in hills to lie and dream
Lulled by the sound of inland stream,
And listening the far soothing moan
Of torrents down the bare crags thrown.

II

But thou hast all unweeting come
Where human joy hath long been dumb.
A land by some strange woe o'ertaken,
Of its own people nigh forsaken,
Where those who linger still retain
Dearth only, penury, and pain,
And wear that uncomplaining [mood]
Which the too long continued stress
Of sore privation hath subdued,
Down to a hopeless passiveness.

III

And this wan sombre afternoon,
That waits the mild rain coming soon,
—A look lies on the loch dead still
As though it felt for human ill,
E'en like a face, so deeply fraught
With brooding and pathetic thought
O'er all of human wrong and woe,
That tears might any hour o'erflow,

And yet such self-control doth keep—
Though on the verge, it will not weep.

IV

But noon is up—bright morn benign—
From sea to summit glad sunshine
This wilderness austere hath thrilled
With grand and wonderous joy—and filled
These mountain faces scarred and riven
With the soft white apparel of heaven.
These peaks, the giant brotherhood,
That round the kinloch [1] crowding brood,
Last night so grey and grim, soar white
And dazzling through the infinite
Blue dome :—what clouds there come and go
Are few and fleecy white as snow.
O joy in such an hour to be
Afloat upon this inland sea
With shore, hills, sky, beneath us seen
To float along two heavens between!
Joy too hath reached the hungry shore :
There now, their small black huts before,
Old bodies sit and sun themselves.
Poor widows pale, with looks refined,
Who through dark winter months have pined
In hunger, each with wasted form

[1] *Kinloch*, lake-head.

Take, while they may, the sunshine warm.
And one or two on rocky shelves
Creep out, to wrench the mussels thence
That to their sea-washed moorings hold,
Not with a clinging more intense
Than they to these bare dwellings old.

V

O region! full of power and change
Of aspect—boundless in thy range
Of gloom and glory, like the soul
Of poet, who takes in the whole,
And renders back what earth hath given
Illumined with the hues of heaven.
Thou hast no mean or common moods!

*   *   *   *   *

And we, who feelingly have been
Partakers of this wondrous scene,
Been rapt in its sublime delight—
Touched with its pathos infinite—
How oft from heartless worldly din
In thought we'll wander back, and win
Refreshment, strength, and calm of tone
From the great vision we have known!
On winter nights will wonder how
It fares up yonder—whether now,

'Mid rain and cloud-drift, these great peaks
Are listening to the night wind's shrieks,
Or, all alone, the blue heaven share
With bright Arcturus or the Bear.

Written July 1871.

PROGNOSTIC

When early morning o'er the mountains high
Had spread a garment of too-brilliant sky,
I've seen mists come from out you knew not where,
From unseen caverns or the cloudless air;
First faintly fleck the flanks, then upward spread
White sheeted swathes around the mountain head:
—Then all the heavens turned to sullen grey,
Came down in floods of rain, and drowned the day.

Written Autumn 1874.

THE WILDERNESS

Up the long corrie, through the screetan [1] rents,
   Past the last cloud-berry and stone-crop flower,
With no companion save the elements,
   This peak of crumbled rock my lone watch-tower,
Bare ridges all around me, weather-bleached,
   Of hoary moss and lichen-crusted stone,
Beyond all sounds of gladness or distress,
   All trace of human feeling—only reached
From far below by the everlasting moan
   The corrie-burns send up, I gaze alone
O'er the wide Ossianic wilderness.

There o'er the abyss by long Loch Ericht cloven,
   Ben-Aulder, huge, broad-breasted,—the heavens bowed
To meet him—hides great shoulders in dark-woven
   And solemn tabernacle of moveless cloud,
And there pavilions 'neath that solid roof
   His deer and eagles, dwelling all alone

---

[1] *Screetan*, stony ravine on mountain-side.

In corrie and cove, inviolately still;
    While with streaks breaking from those skirts
        of woof
His lower flanks he dapples, half-way down,
    Strange visionary dreamings of his own,
That come and go at his mysterious will.

Whence borne we know not, for all heaven is grey,
    And passing hence to go we know not where,
Weary world-wanderers that have lost their way
    On that illimitable moor and bare,
Outcasts disowned by the beclouded sun,
    O'er deer-grass wastes, faint-gleaming, on they
        stray,
Past that one sunless loch so weird and wan,
    To be absorbed in yonder desert dun
That heaves and rolls endlessly north away
    By Corryarrick and the springs of Spey,
The grand old country of the Chattan clan.

Or southward turn—down yonder long defile
    There the great moor of Rannoch darkly looms
From out its clouds and shadows, mile on mile
    Wandering away to ever-deepening glooms
That alway girdle those storm-cradling walls,
    Corriechabah and his huge brethren grim,

While here and there the waste moor shoots some eye
  Of ghostly tarn,[1] and there Loch Loydon crawls,—
A wounded dragon—now in vapours dim
  Enwrapt, and now such lights break over him,
His waters seem a blink of open sky.

That life of clouds and sungleams that doth wage
  Its dusky war athwart this wilderness,
Mid human change unchanging, age on age,
  What poet hath availed to quite express?
Not Donach Bàn,[2] for all his mountain lore.
  Not Walter Scott, though king of minstrel might,
Not even Wordsworth's inspiration strong;
  But he, the voice of Cona, blind and hoar,
Whose youth beheld these movements, and when night,
  Deep night closed on him, by his inward sight
Renewed and clothed them in immortal song.

Ossian is here, and a Being more than he,
  Even that upholding Spirit, who contains

---

[1] *Tarn*, *i.e.* the small loch on the moor.
[2] *Donach Bàn*, Duncan McIntyre, "the Robert Burns of the Highlands."—J. C. S.—See Note at end.

THE WILDERNESS

Within Himself all "kings of melody,"
　All they have sung in their divinest strains;
Nor only these, but all of human souls
　That are, or have been, or shall yet be here,
With all they've known, and all the vast unknown
　Beyond their thought, animates and controls.
To all that moving world close eye and ear!
　For in this awful solitude very near
He cometh to the soul, and He alone.

Written 1874.

THE HIGHLAND RIVER

1

HA! there he comes, the headlong Highland River!
Shout of a king is in his current strong,
Exulting strength that shall endure for ever,
As lashing down his rocks he leaps along.

2

O'er the great boulders, foaming, leaping, bounding
Thy tawny waters from their loch set free!
Thou callest on the sombre hills surrounding,
To come and join in thine exulting glee,

3

Flooding the flats, the rock-barred gorges cleaving,
O'er falls a plunging foaming cataract,
From every brae a tribute-burn receiving,
Brightening with foam the dusky moorland tract.

4

Throb on ! thou heart of this wide wilderness,
The sombre silence with thy gladness fill !
We pass, but Thou remainest,—none the less,
Will throb thy pulses wild, when ours are still.

Written September 1874.

LOST ON SCHIHALLION

SHEPHERD   Oh wherefore cam ye here, Ailie?
                What has brocht you here?
                Late and lane [1] on this bleak muir and eerie,
                A wild place this to be
                For a body frail as ye,
                Wi' the nicht and yon storm-clouds sae near ye.

AILIE   Oh dinna drive me back,
                I canna leave my track,
                Though nicht and the tempest should close o'er me.
                The warld I've left behind,
                And there's nocht I care to find
                Save Schihallion and high heaven that are afore me.

SHEPHERD   Oh speak nae word o' driving,
                But wherefore art thou striving
                For the thing that canna be, puir Ailie?

[1] *Lane*, lone.

                Ye had better far return,
                Where the peat-fires bienly [1] burn,
                And your friends wait ye down at Bohalie.

AILIE   The warld below is cauld and bare,
                Up yonder's the place for prayer;
                There the vision on my soul will break clearer,
                My friends will little miss me,
                And there's only One can bless me,
                To Him on the hill-top I'll be nearer.

SHEPHERD   Schihallion's sides sae sclid [2] and steep,
                And his snow-drifts heap on heap,
                What mortal would dream the nicht [3] o' scaling?
                Gin [4] the heart pray below,
                From nae mountain-top will go
                Your prayer to heaven with cry more prevailing.

AILIE   Weak am I and frail, I ken,
                But there's might that's not of men
                To bear me up—sae na mair entreat me;

---

[1] *Bienly*, cheerfully.   [2] *Sclid*, slippery.
[3] *The nicht*, to-night.   [4] *Gin*, if.

Be the snow-drifts ne'er sae deep,
I have got a tryst to keep
Wi' the angels that up yonder wait to meet
    me.

  * * * * *[1]

The Shepherd home is gone,
And she went on alone ;
Night cam, but she cam not to Bohalie ;
They socht her west and east
Neist day, and then the neist
On Schihallion's head they found puir Ailie.

Stiff with ice her limbs and hair,
And her hands fast closed in prayer,
And her white face to heaven meekly
    turning ;
Down they bore her to her grave,
And they knew her soul was safe
In the home for which sae lang she had
    been yearning.

Written 1874.—A few years ago the incident here alluded to actually occurred, in all its details, in the case of a poor Highland woman, weak in health and of failing mind.

[1] So asterisked when first published.

WILD FLOWERS IN JUNE

I

The showers are over, the skiffing [1] showers,
   Come let us rise and go
Where the happy mountain flowers,
Children of the young June hours,
   In their sweet haunts blow.
Where nor plough nor spade hath clomb,
   On the native upland leas,
Between the heather and the broom
They have made their chosen home,
   Single or in families.

Wet with rain, gleam bell and cup,
   Now the westering sunset lays,
From the valley passing up,
   Splendour on these grassy braes.
Music too, and of the best,
   All about them now is ringing,
For the laverock [2] from her nest
   For even-song is heavenward springing,

[1] *Skiffing*, flying, light.   [2] *Laverock*, lark.

And raining melody in showers
Down upon the lowly flowers.
   And at silent intervals,
While the sunset's round them glistening,
Cometh to their eager listening
   Sound of latest cuckoo-calls
   And of far-off waterfalls.

Lo! the lavish hand of June,
   Far and near, the pasture soil,
Brae and hillock, hath bestrewn
   With a blaze of Bird-trefoil.
And, whene'er you miss its shining,
   See the white and simple sheen
Of the silvery Gallium lining
   All the interspace between:
High and low, the alternate gleam
Of their colours is supreme.

Stoop and see a lowlier kind,
   Creeping Milk-wort, pink, white, blue,
With the hill-bent intertwined,
   Shy, yet hardy, peeping through;
While the Eye-bright twinkles nigh,
With its modest happy eye,
Like one set to bear a gay
Gladsome spirit, come what may.

Here and there on grassy mound
    Thyme and Rock-rose interfuse
On the green knolls they have crowned
    Tender gold with purple hues :
Thyme, within whose odorous beds
    Murmur still late-lingering bees ;
Rock-roses, that droop their heads,
Hastening one by one to fold
Their so delicate discs of gold,
    Ere the sunlight leave the leas.

Coming from you know not where,
    What rich fragrance round us shed !
Suddenly, all unaware,
    Lo ! mid Orchis beds we tread.
Than the odours these bequeath,
    Wildlings of the dry hillside,
Richer none the gardens breathe
    From their pampered flowers of pride.
While their scentless sisters white,
Near them, and those others dight
With a deeper purple wonder,
Down within their moist marsh yonder,
Why to them is disallowed
That which maketh these so proud ?

Where the burn the moor is leaving,
    Ere it leaps the upper linn,

To descend the dark dell cleaving,
   See the light comes slanting in ;
On the heath above the fall,
   There along their favourite haunt,
Yellow Lucken-gowans [1] tall,
   Nothing loth, their splendours flaunt.
All day long in light winds swaying,
Bright eyes they have been displaying ;
Now their globes of gold are furled,
Bidding good-night to the world.

Pass we now across the stream,
   By the margin of the wood
Hidden lies the tenderer gleam
   Of a purer sisterhood.
Wary go—their heathy cover
You may pass, nor once discover,
Underneath, the pure white sheen
Of the starry Winter-green.
Happy flowerets ! stoop and find them,
   They will thrill you with their smile ;
Go your way, and nothing mind them,
   They smile on, and bear no guile.

Now latest lights from topmost heights,
   One by one are fleetly going ;

---

[1] *Lucken-gowan*, Globe-flower, one of the *Ranunculaceae*.

We descend, and homeward wend
   Where white and red wild-roses blowing,
And foxglove bells light the dells ;—
   But we will pass and leave them growing.

II

WINTER-GREEN

(*TRIENTALIS EUROPÆA*)

Darling Flowers ! at last I've found you,
   For so many months unseen,
Through blae-berries clustered round you,
   Twinkling white with starry sheen ;
Flowers to which no equals be
For sweet grace and purity.

As I gaze, O floweret slender !
   Whatsoever things there be,
Spiritual, pure, and tender,
   Rise to thought at sight of thee.
Dweller on this dusky moor,
Meek and humble, bright and pure.

Bright as folding star at even,
   Pure as lamb on vernal lea,

Seeming less of earth than heaven,
    How the heart leaps forth to thee!
Springing from this heathy sod,
Like a thing new-come from God.

With thy pure white petals seven,
    And thy graceful leaflets whorled
Round thy slender stem, brief-living
    Visitant of this rough world,
Thou dost hint at, and foreshow,
What we long for, cannot know.

Though thy soul-like smiles seem foreign
    To our sorrow-clouded clime,
Yet rough wood, and moorland barren,
    Keep thee thy appointed time,
Through all weather, brave to bear
Buffets of our northern air.

Brave to bear, and do thy duty
    Full of cheer; and then depart,
Image of a saint-like beauty
    Leaving with the pure in heart;
All lone places making dear,
Where thy sweet looks re-appear.

Though ye dwell in home secluded,
  Yours is no unsocial mood,
But the beauty unobtruded
  Of a radiant sisterhood,
With your brightness born to bless
Many a bare bleak wilderness.

But howe'er we read your feeling,
  From the world and all its din
Well I know 'tis pleasant stealing
  O'er the desert far to win
Such delight as thrills me through,
Each summer, at first sight of you.

III

Here far removed from garden art,
  Fresh-breaking from the mountain sod,
Your gentle faces touch the heart,
  Like words that come direct from God.

Ye thrill as with a touch so true
  And tender, O ye wildling flowers!
We cannot doubt, Who fashioned you,
  The Same hath made these hearts of ours.

Yes, eyes of beauty bright are ye,
  On human life all soiled and dim
Forth-looking from that central sea
  Of beauty, that abides with Him.

Written 1874.

ALT CUCHIN DOUN

STILL let me dive the glens among,
With birks and rowans [1] overhung;
And wandering up the channel bed
By the burn's wayward windings led,
Exploring every cove, and cool
Recess, each nook, and clear brown pool
With its pure mirror, clear to show
The leaves above, the stones below;
To note each fair fern's various grace,
Each peeping flower's hiding place,
Each lichen-crusted stone and rock,
With dyes so deftly laid,—they mock
All textures of most delicate bloom
E'er wrought on Oriental loom.

With such sweet musings let me stray,
Till some steep cataract bars the way,
Then close my eyes, and let the croon
Of falling waters all attune
My thoughts, and lead to quiet moods
Where no rude worldly thought intrudes,

[1] *Birk*, birch; *rowan*, mountain-ash.

And haply wake within some song
That may the calm sweet hour prolong,
Whate'er it have of pure and fine
To gladden other hearts, as mine.

Written September 12, 1875.

THE SHEPHERD'S HOUSE,

LOCH ERICHT

1

A BOWSHOT from the loch aloof
Beside a burn that sings its tune
All day long to the Shepherd's roof,
Blue smiling through the quiet noon.
Behind it, the long corrie cleaves
A bosom in the Bens, and leaves
These to enfold their wide embrace
Of arms round this lone dwelling-place.

2

Home lonelier, more from kirk and school
Removed is not on Highland ground;
Across the Loch it looketh full
Into Benaulder's coves profound,
And evermore before his broad
And solemn presence overawed,
Receives a too depressing sense
Of Nature's power, man's impotence.

3

Across the Burn its peat-moss lies,
This side, some plats for meadow hay;
Unflagging there the Shepherd plies
His labour all this autumn day,—
He and his dark Lochaber wife,
To store the hay and fuel rife,
This fleeting passing autumn prime
'Gainst snowdrift in this Alpine clime.

4

Hard by, bareheaded, shout and leap
Their lads and lasses at their play;
The clamorous collies yelp to keep
The kye from the kail-yard [1] at bay,
But all these cries, this household din,
Can scarce a faintest echo win
From this vast hush, wherein they seem
No more than sounds far heard in dream.

5

O were this stillness lodged within
The countless hearts in cities pent,
To mitigate the feverish din
With this soul-soothing element;

---

[1] *Kail-yard*, cabbage-garden.

The vext soul's tumult to allay
By thought and quiet having way,
And soothe their pulses' anxious throes
With cool of this profound repose!

6

Yet what is all earth's cities' roar,
The agitation loud and fierce,
That vex her countless hearts, before
The still all-girdling universe?
No more than is the little noise
This household at each day's employs
Makes in the presence of the vast
Absorbing silence round them cast.

Written September 1875.

AUTUMN IN THE HIGHLANDS

OCTOBER[1]

(AFTER KEATS)

I

OCTOBER misty bright, the touch is thine
That the full year to consummation brings,
When noonday suns and nightly frosts combine
To make a glory that outrivals spring's;
The mountain bases swathed in russet fern,
Their middle girths with deer-grass golden-pale,
And the high summits touched with earliest snows
From summer dreamings lift to thoughts more stern;
Then doth the harvest-moon in beauty sail
O'er the far peaks and the mist-steaming vale,
While silver-sheened our household river flows.

II

Who hath not seen thee clambering up the crag,
On sunny days in many-hued attire,
Making wild-cherry leaves thy scarlet flag,

[1] See Note at end.

And kindling rowan boughs to crimson fire?
Sometimes on dizzy rock-ledge thou art seen,
Even as an angel from high heaven new-lit,
Quivering aloft in aspen's pallid gold;
Or far up mountains queen-like thou dost sit,
Cushioned on mosses orange, purple, green,
Or down their bases homeward thou dost lean,
Loaded with withered ferns, a housewife old.

III

What though the summer mountain fruits are gone,
Though of black crowberries grouse have eat their fill?
A few belated cloudberries linger on
High on the moist hill-breast where mists distil;
And now the prickly juniper displays
On dry warm banks his pungent fruitage blue,
Deep in pine-forests wortleberries show
Their box-like leaves and fruit of bright red hue,
And old fail-dykes[1] along the upland braes,
Fringed with blaeberry leaves in scarlet blaze,
Add to October sunsets richer glow.

IV

And for thy songs, home-carting late-won peats,
Crofters low-humming down hill-tracks return,

[1] *Fail-dykes*, walls of turf and stone.

While here and there some lone ewe-mother bleats
Fitfully, for last summer's lamb forlorn ;
O'er heather brown no wild-bee murmurs float,
The pewits gone, shy curlews haste to leave
The high moors where they screamed the summer long ;
From slaughtering guns the mountains win reprieve ;
But still far up on mossy haggs [1] remote
The plover sits and pipes her plaintive note,
And cackling grouse-cock whirs on pinions strong.

GARTH CASTLE [2]

GARTH CASTLE, he hath borne the brunt
    Of twice three hundred years ;
Yet dauntless still his time-rent front
    A ruddy banner rears.

Bethinks he of the blood-red flag,
    Was waving there of old,
When Badenoch's Wolf that island crag
    Chose for his mountain hold ?

On either side a torrent's roar—
    A jaggèd dark ravine—
A headlong precipice before,
    Behind, yon mountain screen,

[1] *Haggs*, see p. 29.   [2] See Note at end.

Here, warder-like, the gorge he keeps,
    Firm foot and aspect grim ;
Schihallion from his mountain steeps
    Looks calmly down on him.

O well he chose this dark defile,
    Who harried far and near,
Fire-wasted Elgin's holy pile,
    And filled these glens with fear.

And then—his work of ravage sped—
    To this stern hold withdrew,
And Scotland's lion, bloody-red,
    From its proud forehead threw.

Those robber chiefs are in their graves,
    And from this ruined brow
A gentler power the red flag waves,
    Not man, but Nature now—

Calm Nature, who these autumn eves
    Her silent finger lays,
And kindles those wild-cherry leaves
    To bright purpureal blaze.

Deft worker ! who like her can rich
    And rare embroidery weave,
To hide the rents of ruin which
    Time's unseen wedges cleave ?

O well for thee ! that thou canst find,
　　After thy stormy day,
A nurse so beautiful and kind
　　To gladden thy decay,

And give to passing hearts to feel
　　How under wrong and ruin
A deep power lies, can gently heal
　　With beautiful renewing.

Written October 1876.

CLATTO[1]

1

Days on days, the East wind blowing
Wind and sleet and blinding rain,
Dark the heavens and darker growing,
Blent in one, sea, hill, and plain.

2

Came a lull, and we ascended
A green hill at close of day,
Whence the heavens' black curtain rended
Showed Schihallion far away

3

Standing out supreme and lonely
O'er the vaporous mirky dim,
With one gleam of sunset only
Slanting down the flanks of him.

4

Brief the vision :—soon we wended
Down to darkness as before ;

[1] In Fife.

And the tempest blowing blended
Sky, and sea, and earth, once more.

5

Drowning haugh[1] and flooding river,
Drenching dark, the storm wind blew
Weary days on days :—will ever
Sun and star again shine through?

6

Yes :—what comfort 'tis to ponder,
Though these vapours dense and chill
Press us down—Schihallion yonder,
In his strength is soaring still.

7

As in happy summers olden
There he stands :—we yet shall see
Spear-like cleave the sunset golden
His peaked forehead,[2] calm and free.

8

So in many a doubtful season,
When the soul's best vision fades,
And no reach of heart or reason
Can pierce through the dull damp shades,

---

[1] *Haugh*, water-meadow.
[2] *His peaked forehead*, see *Schihallion*, p. 128.

9

Strength there is and consolation
Whatsoe'er obstructions hide;
Knowing in their changeless station
Heaven's eternal truths abide.

10

Meek hearts,—who with faith unbating
Through the soul's dark days endure,—
Lights divine for you are waiting;
The great vision is secure!

Written April 21, 1877.

AUCHMORE

O MOUNTAIN stream! so old, yet ever young!
Thy voice so close beside this ancient home
Soothingly murmurs on, for ever on,
Like some old nurse beside a cradled child
Crooning a solemn lullaby; for thou
Wast sounding here long ere this mansion rose,
And wilt be sounding on when it and all
That it inhabit have quite disappeared,
Into the invisible!
     Far up among
The open heathery braes thy springs are born,
And there thou blendest thy first prattle with
The crowing muir-cock and the plover's cry;
Then, on thy journey down, these old pine woods
Receive and solemnize thy plunging roar,
Ere in the lake it is for ever still.
 Unceasingly these waters come and go,
But thou, still voice! for evermore the same
Abidest—sound that does not change or fail,
Eternity in time made audible.
And age by age, fond dwellers here have come,

And loved this house, and listened to this stream
A little while, then gone their unknown way.
And we, who here some passing hours have been,
Falling asleep beneath the lulling sound,
Wakening at morn encompassed still within
The omnipresent murmur, ere we part,
A prayer would breathe for those young hearts,[1] who dwell
From day to day in hearing of this stream,
And call these mountains a brief while their own,
That more than all the noisy jars of time
This monotone so solemn and profound,
This voice so weighted with eternity,
May reach their ears not only, but their souls,
And bear the warning home, with which it comes
Charged from the mountains, of the Eternal One ;—
That they may live to further His great ends,
To whom our hearts are bare, with whom alone
We shall have then to do, when we have passed
Out of the hearing of all earthly sounds.

Written August 4, 1877.

[1] *Those young hearts:* the allusion is to Lord and Lady Breadalbane.

DRUMUACHDAR[1]

TRANSLATION FROM THE GAELIC

O WAE on Loch Laggan!
That bonnie spring day
Lured my lad and his herd
To the desert away:—

Then changed ere night fell
To a demon its form,
And hugged him to death
In the arms of the storm.

Drumuachdar's dark moor
I have wandered in pain;
The herd I have found,
Sought the herdsman in vain.

But my gentle Macdonald
Lay stretched where he fell,
His head on the willow,
His feet in the well.

[1] See Note at end. *Drumuachdar* is pronounced as a trisyllable.

The folk with their dirks
Cutting birches so nigh thee,
O why did none chance
In that hour to pass by thee?

Had I but been there
Ere the death chill had bound thee,
With a dry ample plaid
To fold warmly around thee:

And a quaich [1] of pure spirit
Thrice passed through the reek,[2]
To bring warmth to thy heart,
And the glow to thy cheek.

A bright fire on the floor,
Without smoke or ashes,
In a well woven bothy
Theeked [3] o'er with green rashes.

Not thus, O not thus,
But all lonely thy dying!
Yet the men came in crowds
Where in death thou wast lying.

There was weeping and wail
In the crags to the west of thee,

---

[1] *Quaich*, small drinking-cup.   [2] *Reek*, smoke, fire.
[3] *Theeked*, thatched.

As the race of two grandsires
Came lorn and distressed for thee.

Thy kindred and clansmen
Were mingling their grief,
In the kiln [1] as they laid thee
And waited the chief.

Till Cluny arrived,
His proud head bending low,
Till Clan Vourich arrived,
Each man with his woe.

Till Clan-Ian arrived
To swell the great wail,—
They three that were oldest
And best of the Gael.

With them came too Clan Tavish
The hardiest in fight.
There too were his brothers,
Heart-sick at the sight :

And thy one little sister,
In life's early bloom
Was there too, her beauty
O'ershadowed with gloom.

[1] *Kiln*, see Note at end.

And there stood his old mother
Wringing her hands,
Her grey locks down streaming
Unloosed from their bands.

And the lass of his love
Came riving her hair,
The look of her face
Wild and wan with despair.

O what crying and weeping
That doleful day fills
The hollows and heights
Of Drumuachdar's dark hills!

Written 1878.

LOWLAND LYRICS

THE BUSH ABOON TRAQUAIR

    Will ye gang wi' me and fare
    To the bush aboon[1] Traquair?
Owre the high Minchmuir we'll up and awa',
    This bonny summer noon,
    While the sun shines fair aboon,
And the licht sklents[2] saftly doun on holm and ha'.

    And what would ye do there,
    At the bush aboon Traquair?
A lang driech[3] road, ye had better let it be;
    Save some auld skrunts o' birk[4]
    I' the hill-side lirk,[5]
There's nocht i' the warld for man to see.

    But the blithe lilt o' that air,
    'The Bush aboon Traquair,'
I need nae mair, it's eneuch for me;
    Owre my cradle its sweet chime
    Cam' sughin'[6] frae auld time,
Sae tide what may, I'll awa' and see.

[1] *Aboon*, above.   [2] *Sklents*, slants.   [3] *Driech*, tedious.
[4] *Skrunts o' birk*, ill-grown birches.   [5] *Lirk*, hollow.
[6] *Sughin'*, sighing.

And what saw ye there
At the bush aboon Traquair?
Or what did ye hear that was worth your heed?
I heard the cushies [1] croon
Through the gowden [2] afternoon,
And the Quair burn singing doun to the Vale o' Tweed.

And birks saw I three or four,
Wi' grey moss bearded owre,
The last that are left o' the birken shaw,[3]
Whar mony a simmer [4] e'en
Fond lovers did convene,
Thae bonny bonny gloamins [5] that are lang awa'.

Frae mony a but and ben,[6]
By muirland, holm, and glen,
They cam' ane hour to spen' on the greenwood sward;
But lang hae lad an' lass
Been lying 'neath the grass,
The green green grass o' Traquair kirkyard.

They were blest beyond compare,
When they held their trysting there,
Amang thae greenest hills shone on by the sun;

---

[1] *Cushies*, wood-doves.   [2] *Gowden*, golden.
[3] *Birken shaw*, flat ground at base of hill, overgrown with small birch.   [4] *Simmer*, summer.   [5] *Gloamins*, twilights.
[6] *But and ben*, cottage kitchen and parlour.

And then they wan [1] a rest,
The lownest [2] and the best,
I' Traquair kirkyard when a' was dune.

Now the birks to dust may rot,
Names o' luvers be forgot,
Nae lads and lasses there ony mair convene ;
But the blithe lilt o' yon air
Keeps the bush aboon Traquair,
And the luve that ance was there, aye fresh and green.

This and the five following poems were published in 1864.

[1] *Wan*, won.   [2] *Lownest*, calmest.

THRIEVE CASTLE[1]

WHENCE should ye o'er gentle spirits
    Such o'ermastering power achieve?
Workers of high-handed outrage!
    Making king and people grieve,
O the lawless Lords of Galloway!
    O the bloody towers of Thrieve!

Is it that this time-scarred visage
    From behind five centuries dim,
Doomed to death, yet death-defying,
    Glares the very look of him,
Who first laid these strong foundations,
    Mighty Archibald the Grim?

Impress of those hands is on them,
    That beat Southron foemen down—
Iron hands, that grasped a truncheon
    Weightier than the kingly crown—
Stalwart Earls, broad-browed, black-bearded,
    Pinnacled on power o'ergrown.

[1] See Note at end.

These were they, lone-thoughted builders
   Of yon grim keep, massy-piled,
Triple-walled, and triple-moated,
   In Dee Island triply isled,
O'er the waste of dun morasses,
   Eyeing Cairnsmore mountains wild.

Power gat pride, pride unforgiveness—
   Whoso crossed the moats of Thrieve,
Captive serf, or lordly foeman,
   Though a monarch begged reprieve,
Had they wronged the Lord of Douglas,
   Living ne'er these gates might leave.

Downward! rust in yon dark dungeon
   Rings that once held fettered thrall,
High in air,—the grooved stone gallows
   Ghastly juts from yonder wall,
Where once swung the corse of Bombie,
   Prelude of the Douglas' fall.

Never since from thy scathed forehead
   Hath it passed, the bodeful gloom
Gathered there the hour thy haughtiest
   Lord rode forth, defying doom,
To the monarch's perjured poignard,
   And the deathly banquet room.

Outcast now from human uses,
    Both by war and peace disowned,
All thy high ambitions broken,
    All thy dark deeds unatoned,
Still thou wear'st no meaner aspect,
    Than a despot King dethroned.

Frost and rain, and storm and thunder—
    Time's strong wedges—let them cleave
Breaches through thy solid gables,
    Thou wilt neither blench nor grieve ;
Thou who gav'st, wilt ask, no pity,
    Unrelenting Castle Thrieve !

DEVORGUILLA[1]

OR THE ABBEY OF THE SWEET HEART

In grey Criffel's lap of granite
  Lies the Abbey, saintly fair!
Well the heart, that first did plan it,
  Finds her earthly resting there:

Who from out an age of wildness,
  Lawless force, unbridled crime,
Reachèd forth wise hands in mildness
  Helpful to the coming time.

The rude Galloway chieftain's daughter—
  Memory of her Norman knight,
And long widowed sorrow taught her
  To make good deeds her delight.

Long ere now their names had perished,
  Had not those wise halls,[2] she reared
By the southern Isis, cherished
  Them for Founders' names revered.

---

[1] See Note at end. [2] *Those wise halls*, Balliol College, Oxford.

While these arches o'er Nith river,
    Thronged by daily passers, still
Witness here her pure endeavour
    To complete her dear lord's will.

But for human use or learning
    Good works done, could they appease
Her long heartache? that lone yearning
    Other medicine asked than these.

So she spake, " Rise, page, and ride in
    Haste, this grief will not be calmed,
Till thou from the land he died in
    Bear my dead lord's heart embalmed."

Ivory casket closing round it,
    With enamelled silver, fair
As deft hands could frame, he bound it,
    And with fleet hoofs homeward bare:

Generous heart that once so truly
    With young love for her had beat,
Bore he to her home, and duly
    Laid before the lady's feet.

One whole day her passionate sorrow
    Inly brooded, dark and dumb,
But in silence shaped, the morrow
    Clear as light her words did come.

"Build me here, high-towered and solemn,
    Abbey-church in fairest style,—
Pointed arch, and fluted column,
    Ranged down transept, nave, and aisle."

There the dear heart laid in holy
    Place, the altar-steps before,
Down she knelt herself in lowly
    Adoration on that floor.

Thither day by day she wended,
    On that same spot knelt and prayed;
There at last, when all was ended,
    With the heart she loved was laid.

In that place of ivied ruin
    She hath taken, since the close
Of her life of full well-doing,
    Six long centuries' repose.

Meek one! who, 'mid proud men violent,
    A pure builder unreproved,
Lived and laboured for the silent
    Kingdom that shall ne'er be moved.

THEN AND NOW

A TIME there was,
When this hill-pass,
With castle, keep, and peel,[1]
Stood iron-teethed,
Like warrior sheathed
In mail from head to heel.

Friend or foe,
No man might go,
Out to the English Border,
Nor any ride
To Forth or Clyde,
Unchallenged of the Warder.

At the baron's 'hest
The trooper spurred,
And brought the traveller
Before his lord,
To be dungeon-mured,
Dark, damp, and lone,

---

[1] *Peel*, small square tower in the Border counties.

THEN AND NOW

    Till death had cured
      His weary moan.

But time has pulled the teeth
    From those fierce fangs,
Spread his sward of heath
    O'er the riever[1] gangs;
    Hushed their castles proud,
    As grave-yards still,
    And streamed life loud
    Through mart and mill.

Embowered among green ashes,
    The grey towers sigh, Alas!
As the loud train crashes
    Down the rock-ribbed pass.
    They come and go
    Morn and eve,
    Bear friend and foe,
    And ask no leave.

While the towers look forth
    From their gaunt decay
On an altered earth,
    A strange new day;
    When mechanics pale

[1] *Riever*, robber.

Oust feudal lords,
With wheel and rail,
Not blood-red swords;
And the horny hands
That delve iron-ore,
Grasp mighty lands,
Chiefs ruled of yore.

THE BLUE BELLS

AGAIN the bonny blue bells
   Wave all o'er our dear land,
Or scattered single, here and there,
   Or a numerous sister band.

How many a last leave-taking
   Hath darkened over youthful faces,
Since the hour ye last were here!
   Now in all your wonted places,
From long wintry sleep awaking,
   Blithe ye reappear.

The same ye meet us, be we joyful,
   Or bowed down by heavy loads,
On the thatch of auld clay biggins,[1]
   Shedding grace o'er poor abodes,
Or from dykes [2] of greensward gleaming,
   Hard by unfrequented roads.

O'er the linns of dark Clyde water
   Ye are trembling, from the steep,

[1] *Biggins*, cottages.   [2] *Dykes*, hedge-banks.

And afar on dusky moorlands,
   Where the shepherd wears [1] his sheep,
By the hoary headstone waving
   O'er the Covenanter's sleep.

Ye come ere laverocks [2] cease their singing,
   And abide through sun and rain,
Till our harvest-homes are ended,
   And the barn-yards stored with grain;
Then ye pass, when flock the plover
   To warm lands beyond the main.

In your old haunts, O happy blue bells!
   Ye, when we are gone, shall wave,
And as living we have loved you,
   Dead, one service would we crave,
Come, and in the west winds swinging,
   Prank the sward that folds our grave.

---

[1] *Wears*, leads cautiously to shelter.   [2] *Laverocks*, larks.

THE HAIRST RIG [1]

O HOW my heart lap [2] to her
    Upon the blithe hairst rig!
Ilk [3] morning comin' owre the fur [4]
    Sae gracefu', tall, and trig.

    CHORUS—O the blithe hairst rig!
        The blithe hairst rig;
        Fair fa' the lads and lasses met
        On the blithe hairst rig!

At twal' [5] hours aft we sat aloof,
    Aneth [6] the bielding stook, [7]
And tently [8] frae her bonny loof [9]
    The thistle thorns I took.

When hairst was dune and neebors met
    To haud the canty kirn, [10]
Sae fain [11] we twa to steal awa'
    And daunder up the burn.

---

[1] *Hairst Rig*, harvest field at reaping-time.   [2] *Lap*, leapt.
[3] *Ilk*, each.   [4] *Fur*, furrow.   [5] *Twal'*, noon.
[6] *Aneth*, beneath.   [7] *Bielding stook*, sheltering sheaves set up against each other.   [8] *Tently*, deftly.   [9] *Loof*, open hand.
[10] *Haud the canty kirn*, keep the cheerful harvest home.
[11] *Fain*, longing.

The lammies white as new-fa'en drift,
    Lay quiet on the hills,
The clouds aboon i' the deep blue lift,[1]
    Lay whiter, purer still.

Ay, pearly white, the clouds that night
    Shone marled[2] to the moon,
But nought like you, my bonny doo!
    All earth or heaven aboon.

The burnie whimpering siller[3] clear,
    It made a pleasant tune;
But O! there murmured in my ear
    A sweeter holier soun'.

Lang, lang we cracked,[4] and went and came,
    And daundered, laith[5] to part;
But the ae thing I daured na name
    Was that lay neist my heart.

Fareweel cam' owre and owre again,
    And yet we could na sever,
Till words were spake in that dear glen,
    That made us ane forever.

---

[1] *Lift*, sky.   [2] *Marled*, chequered.   [3] *Siller*, silver.
[4] *Cracked*, chatted.   [5] *Laith*, loath.

MANOR WATER

1

Doth Yarrow flow endeared by dream
And chaunt of Bard and Poet?
As fair to sight flows Manor's stream,
And only shepherds know it:—

2

In autumn time when thistle down
Upon the breeze is sailing,
And from high clouds the shadows brown
Go o'er the mountains trailing.

3

The streams of Yarrow do not range
By greener holm or meadow,
Nor win a sweeter interchange
Of sunshine and of shadow.

4

And when along these heights serene
Go days of autumn weather,
How splendid then the grassy sheen
With bracken blent and heather.

5

When from yon hill across the glen
The Harvest moon doth wander,
She lingers o'er no strath or Ben
With sweeter looks and fonder.

6

Then what hath Yarrow, that famed stream
By hundred Poets chaunted,
To win the glory and the dream
This dale hath wholly wanted?

7

It is not beauty, nor rich store
Of braver deeds and older:
Down all this water Peel towers hoar
Of stern old warriors moulder.

8

O'er these hills rode beneath the moon
With his Bride, Lord William[1] flying;
At this wan water they lighted down,
The stream his life blood dyeing.

---

[1] *Lord William*, see "The Douglas Tragedy," in Scott's *Minstrelsy of the Scottish Border*.

9

Whence then did Yarrow win her claim
To such poetic favour?
She kept the old melodious name,
The old Celtic people gave her.

10

And when upon her banks befell
Some love-pain, or deep sorrow,
Some Bard was nigh to sing it well,
To the magic chime of Yarrow.

Written about 1867.

SONG OF THE SOUTH COUNTREE

1

O THE Border Hills sae green
I' the South Countree!
With the heather streaked between
In the South Countree!
Sae blythe as I hae been,
Sic sights as I hae seen,
Wide wandering morn to e'en
In the South Countree!

2

And it's all enchanted ground
I' the South Countree;
Fairy knowe and moated mound
On hill, and holm, and lea;
Grey stannin[1] stane and barrow
Of old chiefs by Tweed and Yarrow
I' the South Countree.

[1] *Stannin*, standing.

3

When gloamin' grey comes down
I' the South Countree,
And the hills look weird and brown
I' the South Countree,
High up the grey mists sail,
And, beneath, the river pale
Winds lonely down the dale,
I' the South Countree.

4

At foot of hope [1] and glen,
In the South Countree
Moulder Peels [2] of stalwart men
I' the South Countree;
But quenched their day of pride
When they warned the water [3] wide,
'Gainst their foes to rise and ride
Frae the South Countree.

5

And looks of beauty rare
I' the South Countree,

---

[1] *Hope*, sloping valley between mountain-ridges.
[2] *Peels*, Border-towers.
[3] *Warned the water*, summoned allies along the river.

Went smiling up the stair
In the South Countree,
When Mary, Yarrow's flower,
Looked forth through shine and shower
From Dryhope's lonely Tower
In the South Countree.

6

Yet though the towers down fa'
I' the South Countree,
There are winsome flowers that blaw
I' the South Countree!
O sae happy would I be
With her that's dear to me,
There to live, and there to dee,
I' the South Countree.

Written 1867.

THREE FRIENDS[1] IN YARROW

ADDRESSED TO E. L. LUSHINGTON

1

O MANY a year is gone, since in life's fresh dawn,
    The bonny forest over,
Morn to eve I wandered wide, as blithe as ever bride
    To meet her faithful lover.

2

From Newark's birchen bower, to Dryhope's hoary
    Tower,
    Peel and Keep I traced and numbered;
And sought o'er muir and brae, by cairn and cromlech grey,
    The graves where old warriors slumbered.

3

Where'er on hope or dale has lingered some faint
    trail
    Of song or minstrel glory,

[1] See Note at end.

There I drank deep draughts at will, but could never
    drink my fill,
    Of the ancient Border story.

4

O fond and foolish time, when to ballad and old
    rhyme
    Every throb of my pulse was beating!
As if old world things like these could minister
    heart-ease,
    Or the soul's deep want be meeting!

*   *   *   *   *[1]

5

Now when gone is summer prime, and the mellow
    autumn time
    Of the year and of life has found us,
With Thee, O gentle friend, how sweet one hour to
    spend,
    With the beauty of Yarrow all around us!

6

With him too for a guide, the Poet of Tweedside,
    Our steps 'mong the braes to order,
Who still doth prolong the fervour, torrent-strong;
    The old spirit of the Border.

[1] So asterisked in MS.

7

Heaven's calm autumnal grey on holm and hillside
    lay,
  With here and there a gleaming ;
As the glints of sunny sheen down Herman's [1] slopes
    of green
  O'er St. Mary's Lake came dreaming.

8

There on Dryhope's Tower forlorn we marked the
    rowan, born
  From the rents of roofless ruin ;
And heard the [bridal] tale of the Flower of Yarrow
    Vale,[2]
  And her old romantic wooing.

9

And then we wandered higher, where once St. Mary's
    quire
  O'er the still Lake watch was keeping :
But nothing now is seen save the lonely hillocks
    green,
  Where the Shepherds of Yarrow are sleeping.

---

[1] *Herman* Law, hill marking the watershed between Yarrow and Moffat waters.   [2] See Note at end.

10

And we stood by the stone where Piers Cockburn [1]
    rests alone,
  With his Bride in their dwelling narrow ;
And thou heard'st their tale of dool, and the wail of
    sorrow full,
  The saddest ever wailed on Yarrow.

11

Thou didst listen, while thine eye all lovingly did lie
  On the green braes spread around thee ;
But I knew by the deep rapt quiet thou didst keep,
  That the power of Yarrow had bound thee.

12

O well that Yarrow should put on her sweetest mood
  To meet thy gentle being ;
For of both the native mien and the fortunes ye have
    seen,
  Respond with a strange agreeing.

13

There was beauty here before sorrow swept the Forest
    o'er,
  Its beauty more meek to render :—

---

[1] See Note at end.

Thou wert gentle from thy birth, and the toils and
    cares of earth
  Have but made thee more wisely tender.

14

High souls have come and gone, and on these braes
    have thrown
  The light of their glorious fancies,
And left their words to dwell and mingle with the
    spell
  Of a thousand old romances.

15

And who more fit to find, [than] thou, in soul and mind
  All akin to great bards departed,—
The high thoughts here they breathed, the boon they
    have bequeathed
  To all the tender hearted?

16

And we who did partake, by still St. Mary's Lake,
  Those hours of renewed communion,
Shall feel when far apart, the remembrance at our
    heart
  Keeps alive our foregone soul-union.

17

From this world of eye and ear soon we must disappear;
    But our after-life may borrow
From these scenes some tone and hue, when all things are made new
    In a fairer land than Yarrow.

Written September 1878.

CHARACTER PIECES

BALLIOL SCHOLARS

1840–1843

A REMEMBRANCE

1

WITHIN the ancient College-gate I passed,
   Looked round once more upon the well-known
      square :
Change had been busy since I saw it last,
   Replacing crumbled walls by new and fair ;
The old chapel gone—a roof of statelier show
Soared high—I wondered if it sees below
   As pure heart-worship, as confiding prayer.

2

But though walls, chapel, garden, all are changed,
   And through these courts quick generations fleet,
There are whom still I see round table ranged,
   In chapel snowy-stoled for matins meet ;

Though many faces since have come and gone,
Changeless in memory these still live on,
   A Scholar brotherhood, high-souled, complete.

3

From old foundations where the nation rears
   Her darlings, came that flower of England's youth
And here in latest teens, or riper years,
   Stood drinking in all nobleness and truth.
By streams of Isis 'twas a fervid time,
When zeal and young devotion held their prime,
   Whereof not unreceptive these in sooth.

4

The voice that weekly from St. Mary's spake,[1]
   As from the unseen world oracular,
Strong as another Wesley, to re-wake
   The sluggish heart of England, near and far,
Voice so intense to win men, or repel,
Piercing yet tender, on these spirits fell,
   Making them other, higher than they were.

5

Foremost one stood, with forehead high and broad,[2]—
   Sculptor ne'er moulded grander dome of thought,—
Beneath it, eyes dark-lustred rolled and glowed,

---

[1] J. H. (Cardinal) Newman.   [2] Arthur H. Clough.

Deep wells of feeling where the full soul wrought ;
Yet lithe of limb, and strong as shepherd boy,
He roamed the wastes and drank the mountain joy,
    To cool a heart too cruelly distraught.

6

The voice that from St. Mary's thrilled the hour,
    He could not choose but let it in, though loath ;
Yet a far other voice with earlier power [1]
    Had touched his soul and won his first heart-troth,
In school-days heard, not far from Avon's stream : [2]
Anon there dawned on him a wilder dream,
    Opening strange tracts of thought remote from both.

7

All travail pangs of thought too soon he knew,
    All currents felt, that shake these anxious years,
Striving to walk to tender conscience true,
    And bear his load alone, nor vex his peers.
From these, alas ! too soon he moved apart ;
Sorrowing they saw him go, with loyal heart,
    Such heart as greatly loves, but more reveres.

8

Away o'er Highland Bens and glens, away
    He roamed, rejoicing without let or bound.

---

[1] Dr. Arnold.   [2] Rugby.

And, yearning still to vast America,
   A simpler life, more freedom, sought, not found.
Now the world listens to his lone soul-songs;
But he, for all its miseries and wrongs
   Sad no more, sleeps beneath Italian ground.

9

Beside that elder scholar one there stood,[1]
   On Sunday mornings 'mid the band white-stoled,
As deep of thought, but chastened more of mood,
   Devout, affectionate, and humble-souled.
There, as he stood in chapel, week by week,
Lines of deep feeling furrowing down his cheek
   Lent him, even then, an aspect strangely old.

10

Not from the great foundations of the land,
   But from a wise and learnèd father's roof,
His place he won amid that scholar band,
   Where finest gifts of mind were put to proof;
And if some things he missed which great schools teach,
More precious traits he kept, beyond their reach,—
   Shy traits that rougher world had scared aloof.

[1] Rev. Constantine Prichard.

11

Him early prophet souls of Oriel
  A boy-companion to their converse drew,
And yet his thought was free, and pondered well
  All sides of truth, and gave to each its due.
O pure wise heart, and guileless as a child!
In thee, all jarring discords reconciled,
  Knowledge and reverence undivided grew.

12

Ah me! we dreamed it had been his to lead
  The world by power of deeply-pondered books,
And lure a rash and hasty age to heed
  Old truths set forth with fresh and winsome looks;
But he those heights forsook for the low vale
And sober shades, where dwells misfortune pale,
  And sorrow pines in unremembered nooks.

13

Where'er a lone one lay and had no friend,
  A son of consolation there was he;
And all life long there was no pain to tend,
  No grief to solace, but his heart was free;
And then, his years of pastoral service done,
And his long suffering meekly borne, he won
  A grave of peace by England's southern sea.

14

More than all arguments in deep books stored,
   Than any preacher's penetrative tone,
More than all music by rapt poet poured,
   To have seen thy life, thy converse to have known,
Was witness for thy Lord—that thus to be
Humble, and true, and loving, like to thee—
   This was worth living for, and this alone.

15

Fair-haired and tall, slim, but of stately mien,[1]
   Inheritor of a high poetic name,
Another, in the bright bloom of nineteen,
   Fresh from the pleasant fields of Eton came:
Whate'er of beautiful or poet sung,
Or statesman uttered, round his memory clung;
   Before him shone resplendent heights of fame.

16

With friends around the board, no wit so fine
   To wing the jest, the sparkling tale to tell;
Yet ofttimes listening in St. Mary's shrine,
   Profounder moods upon his spirit fell:
We heard him then, England has heard him since,

[1] J. D. (Lord) Coleridge.

Uphold the fallen, make the guilty wince,
    And the hushed Senate have confessed the spell.

17

There too was one, broad-browed, with open face,[1]
    And frame for toil compacted—him with pride
A school of Devon [2] from a rural place
    Had sent to stand these chosen ones beside;
From childhood trained all hardness to endure,
To love the things that noble are, and pure,
    And think and do the truth, whate'er betide.

18

With strength for labour, "as the strength of ten,"
    To ceaseless toil he girt him night and day;
A native king and ruler among men,
    Ploughman or Premier, born to bear true sway;
Small or great duty never known to shirk,
He bounded joyously to sternest work,—
    Less buoyant others turn to sport and play.

19

Comes brightly back one day—he had performed
    Within the Schools some more than looked-for feat,
And friends and brother scholars round him swarmed

---

[1] Frederick Temple (Bishop of London).   [2] Tiverton School.

To give the day to gladness that was meet :
Forth to the fields we fared,—among the young
Green leaves and grass, his laugh the loudest rung ;
    Beyond the rest his bound flew far and fleet.

20

All afternoon o'er Shotover's breezy heath
    We ranged, through bush and brake instinct with
        spring,
The vernal dream-lights o'er the plains beneath
    Trailed, overhead the skylarks carolling ;
Then home through evening-shadowed fields we went,
And filled our College rooms with merriment,—
    Pure joys, whose memory contains no sting.

21

And thou wast there that day, my earliest friend [1]
    In Oxford ! sharer of that joy the while !
Ah me, with what delightsome memories blend
    " Thy pale calm face, thy strangely-soothing smile ;"
What hours come back, when, pacing College walks,
New knowledge dawned on us, or friendly talks
    Inserted, long night-labours would beguile.

        [1] J. Billingsly Seymour.

22

What strolls through meadows mown of fragrant hay,
  On summer evenings by smooth Cherwell stream,
When Homer's song, or chaunt from Shelley's lay,
  Added new splendour to the sunset gleam:
Or how, on calm of Sunday afternoon,
Keble's low sweet voice to devout commune,
  And heavenward musings, would the hours redeem.

23

But when on crimson creeper o'er the wall
  Autumn his finger beautifully impressed,
And came, the third time at October's call,
  Cheerily trooping to their rooms the rest,
Filling them with glad greetings and young glee,
His room alone was empty—henceforth we
  By his sweet fellowship no more were blest.

24

Too soon, too quickly from our longing sight,
  Fading he passed, and left us to deplore
From all our Oxford day a lovely light
  Gone, which no after morning could restore.
Through his own meadows Cherwell still wound on,
And Thames by Eton fields as glorious shone—
  He who so loved them would come back no more.

25

Among that scholar band the youngest pair [1]
  In hall and chapel side by side were seen,
Each of high hopes and noble promise heir,
  But far in thought apart—a world between.
The one wide-welcomed for a father's fame,
Entered with free bold step that seemed to claim
  Fame for himself, nor on another lean.

26

So full of power, yet blithe and debonair,
  Rallying his friends with pleasant banter gay,
Or half a-dream chaunting with jaunty air
  Great words of Goethe, catch of Béranger.
We see the banter sparkle in his prose,
But knew not then the undertone that flows,
  So calmly sad, through all his stately lay.

27

The other of an ancient name, erst dear
  To Border Hills, though thence too long exiled,
In lore of Hellas scholar without peer,
  Reared in grey halls on banks of Severn piled:
Reserved he was, of few words and slow speech,

[1] Matthew Arnold and James Riddell.

But dwelt strange power, that beyond words could reach,
 In that sweet face by no rude thought defiled.

28

Oft at the hour when round the board at wine,
 Friends met, and others' talk flowed fast and free,
His listening silence and grave look benign
 More than all speech made sweet society.
But when the rowers, on their rivals gaining,
Close on the goal bent, every sinew straining—
 Then who more stout, more resolute than he?

29

With that dear memory come back most of all
 Calm days in Holy Week together spent;
Then brightness of the Easter Festival
 O'er all things streaming, as a-field we went
Up Hincksey vale, where gleamed the young primroses,
And happy children gathered them in posies,
 Of that glad season meet accompaniment.

30

Of that bright band already more than half
 Have passed beyond earth's longing and regret;
The remnant, for grave thought or pleasant laugh,

Can meet no longer as of old they met:
Yet, O pure souls! there are who still retain
Deep in their hearts the high ideal strain
    They heard with you, and never can forget.

31

To have passed with them the threshold of young life,
    Where the man meets, not yet absorbs the boy,
And, ere descending to the dusty strife,
    Gazed from clear heights of intellectual joy,
That an undying image left enshrined,
A sense of nobleness in human kind,
    Experience cannot dim, nor time destroy.

32

Since then, through all the jars of life's routine,
    All that down-drags the spirit's loftier mood,
I have been soothed by fellowship serene
    Of single souls with heaven's own light endued.
But look where'er I may—before, behind—
I have not found, nor now expect to find,
    Another such high-hearted brotherhood.

Published March 1873.

DEAN STANLEY AT ST. ANDREWS

GUEST! but no stranger,—many a time before
Thy feet had turned with fervour all thine own,
To pace our lost Cathedral's grass-grown floor,
Through skeleton walls and altars overthrown;
To trace dim graves where saint and martyr sleep,
Or wander where wild moor and sea-washed keep
Saw mitred heads, by bloody hands struck down.

Long lay these memories blank to common eyes,
Waiting their Poet :—thy voice ringing clear,
Pealed through our halls—the buried shades arise,
The strifes of former centuries re-appear,
And mighty names historic, in long line,
Starting to life, before our vision shine,
Majestic, as they moved in presence here.

Passed soon that thrilling hour: and we too pass
But that fine strain of wisdom shall not flee
Transient as shadows over summer grass,
But dwell, we trust, in many a heart, and be
A power benign, for good that shall endure,

A spring of aspiration high and pure,
Of large forbearance and sweet courtesy.

Those stirring tones, their every rise and fall,—
That vivid countenance, that winning mien,
Some youth to listening ears shall yet recall
In far days on, when we no more are seen ;
" Stanley's voice long ago, like trumpet call,
I heard it thrill St. Andrews' antique hall,—
None other such have heard through all the years
    between."

St. Salvator's College, St. Andrews, 19th April 1875.

THE DEATH OF PRINCE·ALBERT

These hoary, dialed, belfry Towers
Have counted many centuries' hours,
   But never tolled so doleful chime,
As that slow, solemn knell to-day
They pealed for him just passed away,
   The Prince laid low in manhood's prime.

It thrills through every tower and town,
From where the cliffs of Dover frown,
   To far Orcadian headlands rolled,
Saddening the people, high and low,
From hall to humblest hut, as though
   In every home one heart were cold.

All mourn with her who wears the crown,
Bowed in a lonelier sorrow down,
   Than any mourner in the land,
Weeping above his darkened dust,
To whom she leaned in love and trust,
   The strong stay of her sceptred hand.

Well may she mourn, so humbly great
He stood beside her, unelate,
   Lending the might true wisdom lends,
Far-reaching thought, truth-tempered will,
And upward aim, yet calm and still
   To guide the State to noble ends.

How lofty and benign his course!
From vain self-seeking, harmful force,
   And splendid idlesse, all removed!
Pure in himself, and toward the pure
Serene things, that alone endure,
   Still labouring, stedfast, unreproved.

But that cold voice!—through palace gate
It passed, unchallenged, guards that wait
   Around those portals night and day;
Passed on, unheard, by page and groom,
Pierced to that stately, silent room,
   And coldly whispered, "come away."

We start, as though noon-day, that shone
A moment since, were quenched and gone;
   Falls dim eclipse the land athwart,
And, only now thy head is low,
These islands in their sorrow know
   The all thou wert, O princely heart!

St. Andrews, December 1861.

ON THE DEATH OF

SIR JAMES SIMPSON, Bart. M.D.

HATH then that life-long combatant with death,
He who so oft the tyrant foiled,
Who stayed for many, a while, their fleeting breath,
Sunk of his might despoiled?

Ah! Yes! that native strength of nerve and brain
Wrested from powers till then unknown
The marvellous anodyne [1] for others' pain,
But found none for his own.

Thousands in every land beneath the sun
Will hear that word, and, hearing, grieve,
The head is low that for the sufferer won
So gracious a reprieve.

Hath God then sat behind the clouds and heard
The helpless generations groan
Through all those ages, by no pity stirred,
How much soe'er they moan—

[1] Chloroform.

He, Who by one small fiat of His will,
One move of His Almighty hand,
Could bid all human agony be still,
And sorrow countermand?

Is man so pitiful, our God so hard,
Doth the weak labour to relieve
Weak fellow-man, the strong have no regard,
How much soe'er they grieve?

In the great fountain whence that pity came,
The thought that filled that mortal mind,
Is there not, unexhausted, of the same
Large residue behind?

Not coldly contemplating human pain
In highest Heaven He sits aloof,
But stoops Himself to bear the stress and strain,
And puts His Love to proof.

For He the winepress red with anguish trod,
And let the Father's heart shine through
As not impassive—but a suffering God,
With whom we have to do.

To combat with our spiritual foes
He from the height of heaven descends,

ON THE DEATH OF SIR JAMES SIMPSON

Down to the lowest depth, and counts
Who will to follow, Friends.

And not alone for those few human years
He underwent our load of ill,
But all the days of old He bore, and bears
The whole world's burden still.

O mystery of evil! Whence it came
What thought can fathom,—yet we know
He strives man's desolation to reclaim,
And counterwork our woe.

And they, throughout all time, who have wrought
    in love
For human kind, form one great band
Of brother workers, in forefront of which,
Chief worker, Christ doth stand.

Written 1870.

SPRING, 1876

1

No softer south than this did ever fall,
The calmèd heavens no gentler look e'er cast,
On wakening earth through any spring time, all
    The generations past.

2

This is the season that through Chaucer's veins
'Mid England's woods, a thrill of gladness sent ;
The same with Wordsworth's most ethereal strains
    'Mid his own mountains blent.

3

Yet all spring-melodies of bards have voiced
How small a moiety of the mighty sum,
Wherewith, in past Springs, countless hearts rejoiced
    In gladness deep, though dumb.

4

Season of hope they named thee—fondly dreamed
Thou wert the pledge of fairer hours to be—
Hath any summer e'er that pledge redeemed
    To poor humanity?

5

And we whose hearts erewhile when Spring came
    round
With hearts of friends for joy were wont to leap,
Think how to-day Spring touches many a mound,
    'Neath which those loved ones sleep!

6

One[1] rests, ah dearest! by Tay's lucent wave,
Under a great crag's overshadowing brow,
To Christ unseen his pure strong life he gave—
    We trust he sees Him now.

7

And One,[2]—beneath roars factory, forge, and mart!
Above—the still green fell, and boyhood's glen,—
There rests o'erwearied that large human heart,
    That brother man of men.

[1] Henry Alexander Douglas: [2] Norman Macleod:—See Note at end.

8

Can we, for whom the face of earth is filled
So full of graves, on Spring look any more,
And entertain the vernal hopes that thrilled
    Our hearts in springs of yore?

9

Therefore we will not take these vernal moods
For promise of sure earthly good to be;
We will not go to cull through budding woods
    The frail anemone.

10

Rather to us shall all this floral sheen,
That breadth of wood so fresh, so lustrous-leaved,
Hint of a beauty that no eye hath seen,
    No human heart conceived.

HIGHLAND STUDENTS[1]

I[2]

BEYOND the bay, beyond the gleaming sands,
This Sabbath eve, that sunset from the bank
Of clouds down-breaking on yon Highland hills
Is gilding there, I wot, the new-made grave
Of one we knew and loved. But two days gone,
In an old mountain kirk-yard, underneath
The great Schihallion, by a full-flowing stream,
They happed the green sward o'er his noble head;
And that was all of him. Five years agone,
When the chill autumn, by the waning birks
And the wa-gang[3] o' the swallow, warned us down
From summering on the hills to winter work,
In the clachan[4] by the loch-side came to us
A Highland matron, gentle, tall, and pale;
And in sweet Celtic tone spake of her son.
"Her only boy, her Duncan, he was bound

[1] See Note at end.   [2] Duncan Campbell.
[3] *Wa-gang*, departure.   [4] *Clachan*, village.

In a few weeks for college. He had been
An eident[1] learner in the village school,
Much honoured by the teacher. To themselves
Kind son he was, and alway dutiful;
Sparing himself no labour, so he might
Lighten their burden. Now his heart was set
On finding better learning, they would do
Their best to help him through his student years."
And then she ceased, commending him to me.

Soon as November opened college doors,
Young Duncan entered: tall and strong, like one
Who had seen hardness, and was fit for more.
His countenance and mien bespoke a heart
True to the core as sturdiest Lowlander's,
Yet sweetened more than Lowland manners are
By the fine courtesy of the ancient Gael.
Each winter morn I saw him in his place,
Between two students of the same clan-name:
One, scion of a house renowned of old;
The other humbler. As he sat and heard
The lore of Rome unrolled, his listening mind
Drank, and expanded as the daisied bank
Spreads to the sun in May-time. When spring brought
Once more the early swallows, home he hied

[1] *Eident*, diligent.

To his own mountains, bearing back withal
A good report, and a fair scholar's name.
That summer tide on a bleak mountain edge
I found my student; he had doffed the gown
For the rough mason's gear, to labour there
A-dyking with his father. All day long
They built those dry-stone walls that miles and miles
Cross ridgy backs of hills, to part sheep farms
Or lands of neighbouring lairds. In that lone place
How cheery was his greeting! while he told
How there he wrought the solid day, and saved
What margin might be won from morn or eve
For book-work. Something of his history more
That time I learnt, 'mid his own people—how
In a sequestered place, where no school was,
An old clay cottage he had made his school,
And taught the children of the shepherds with
Those of poor crofters. If a shepherd lad
In all that country wished to mend his lore,
He had recourse to Duncan. I have talked
Upon the autumn braes with youths whose thought
For clearness made me marvel, and I found
That they had been with him. In every home,
From high Brae-Lyon all down Tummel, he
For his well-doing had an honoured name.
Three following winters he returned, and gleaned
What lore our college yields, and from all hearts,

Both those who taught and those who learned with him,
Earned not less honour than on Rannochside.
But neither learning nor esteem of men
Aught changed his nature's strong simplicity.
How oft o' nights, when nor'-winds from the sea
Howled round our gables, hath he sat and cheered
Our hearth with legends from the hills!—wild tales
Of ghostly voices heard up Doirie-vhor,
And wandering people from their senses frayed,
By the weird lochan.[1] Sometimes would he bring
Snatches of ancient song, in summer gleaned
From hoary men—wild Celtic melodies—
In long Glen Lyon, or by lone Loch Treig,
For ages sung, but now, like morning mists,
From the glens disappearing.

                         When the time
Had come that he must crown with a degree
His four years' toil, the struggle was severe,—
But the end was honour, and a good reward.
And then the goal that he had looked to long—
The Christian ministry—seemed almost won.
But God had willed he should not touch that goal.
Scarce had he entered on the untried field
Of Hebrew learning, when or toils foregone,

[1] *Lochan*, diminutive of *loch*.

Or new work underta'en for self-support,
Or for the old folk at home, so wore him that
He other seemed than the Duncan that we knew.
Last yule came bitter chill, and fierce-fanged winds
Seized his strong frame, and with joint-racking rheums
Stretched him on bed of pain for many days.
With Spring we saw him creeping out once more,
But with sunk cheek and feeble; yet we said
Summer on his own mountains meeting him
Will breathe the health back Winter hath brought low.
But he had other warnings,—chilling faints
That said these hopes were vain; and yet through all
He bore a cheerful heart. But that last morn
Just ere he left the old collegiate town,
He grasped his best friend by the hand, and said,
"I know that I return no more." The day
He journeyed home was cold, a biting wind
Smote him, and when he entered the old home
It only was to lay him down and die.
Through weary weeks of struggle that remained,
Mother and one sole sister tended him
Their best—did what poor human love will do;
But ere the longest day came, that dear life—
Joy of their hearts, their one sole hope on earth—
Faded before them into eternity.
And now Schihallion's shadow on his grave
Rests, and morn smites and night pavilions there

High over-head, and the river roars beneath.
But what to him these mountain pageantries ?
And what to them, poor hearts ! that pine hard by,
Whom spring or summer can make glad no more ?
Yet, O ye mourners ! though ye needs must go
Lorn for him all your days—a little while
In faith hold on, and ye shall see him, where
For them found faithful in a few things here
There yet remain the many things of God !

Published 1867.

II [1]

The mighty shadow which Schihallion flings
To nor'ward, falls athwart a hillock green,
A steep green knoll, with one sole elm-tree crowned,
And a forsaken place of burial.
Thither,—before the turf on Duncan's grave,
Yonder, the other side of Tummel stream,
Had knit itself with green,—a student-friend
Was carried to his last lone resting-place.
Climb we the knoll so steep and green, to see
The small kirkyard, along the smooth top spread,
Its roofless long-abandoned chapelry,
And mossed wall crumbling round it. There they lie,
Under rough mountain slabs, without a name,

[1] Ewan Cameron.

By tall weeds overgrown, the old Rannoch men,
Stewarts, Macgregors, Camerons. On one side,
Beneath the spread of that great elm-tree's boughs,
A headstone gleams more than the rest adorned,
That marks the grave of Ewan Cameron.
Here sit we down upon the lichened wall,
The while I tell thee all the brief sad tale,
Brief, but not sad, of the young sleeper there.
Natives of this same strath these lads were born,
To the same college student-friends they came.
Yonder their homes lie, scarce a mile between,
Duncan's within the clachan by the loch,
Ewan's, that farmstead 'neath the bielding hill,
In trees half-hid. ·Now half a mile apart
Lie their two graves, the river flowing between.
Poor was his farm, not numerous the flock
That Ewan's father on that mountain fed,
And only with sore struggle he prevailed
'Gainst pressure of hard times to hold his own,
And rear his children, sheltering from toil
The tender youth of Ewan, eldest born.
His parents, grave and serious, held the faith
Of a small remnant of religious men,
Living in households sprinkled near and far
Among the glens. In dawn of life from these,
Their strict home ways, their Sabbath pieties,
Ewan had drunk a stern and fervid faith,

Yet tempered well by native gentleness.
For very gentle he was, with open heart
To kindly nature. In the village school
On the same bench by Duncan's side he sat,
Was taught by the same master. School hours o'er,
They took the Braes together, ranged at will
The ample folds of broad Benchualach,
Guddling[1] for trouts far up the mountain burns,
And gathering wortles and ripe blaeberries,
High on the heights where the red gor-cock crowed,
Against the scarlet clouds by sunset flamed
Back from Ben Aulder and the peaks that crowd
Far westward to Ben Nevis. That free life
Had mellowed whatsoe'er austerity
Might else have been engendered. When he came
With Duncan to the old collegiate town,
Beneath the college archway ne'er had passed
A comelier lad. His tall and shapely form
And easy carriage showed him strange to toil,
But on his thoughtful brow and clear pale cheek
Rested a shadow, as of pain foregone.
Whene'er you spoke to him, you were aware
Of a calm dignity and natural grace,
Brought whence you knew not, that was finer far
Than any gathered in the polished world.
When he conversed with men, his manners wore

[1] *Guddling*, groping.

A mild reserve; but soon as he addressed
A lady, through his mien and words there shone
A high-born courtesy, had well beseemed
The gentle Cameron of the "Forty-five."

Two winters he abode with us. Even now
I seem to see him in the college room,
In his appointed place, with intense look,
Quick to respond to aught of higher mood
As a hill-lochan on a serene day
To take the gleams and shadows. To that seat
How many faces since have come and gone,
But none of all so filled with repressed fire,
And reverent thought, and grave sweet purity.

A shorter space Ewan remained with us
Than Duncan did; and his health less robust
And shyer spirit made him more withdraw
From the outer world, and shelter him within
A smaller circle. But on these his friends
He turned a side of winning gentleness,
Which they gave back with a peculiar love.
Hence he passed southward to an English hall,
Where his own people reared their ministers;
And then, his years of preparation done,
Came forth a preacher, not in his own glens
To native Celtic clansmen, but far south,

In low, dull flats, beside the streams of Don,
'Mid Yorkshire factory folk to minister,
A stranger amid strangers.   But few weeks
Passed, ere the warm thrill of a living faith,
Streamed through his Celtic fervour eloquent,
Had touched the tough but honest Yorkshire hearts
And drawn them all towards him.   It befell,
One sultry day in the midsummer tide,
When he had made a trysting to address
The people gathered 'neath the open sky,
And speak of things divine, he missed the train,
And five miles ran afoot to keep his tryst.
Then a long hour, o'er-heated, on a mound
He stood bare-headed, pleading earnestly—
So very earnestly—for eternal things,
He heeded not the accidents of time.
Next morn strong fever had him in its grasp,
And a short space sufficed to bring him low,
So low that they who watched said, "We write
To call your mother hither."—" No," he said,
" A few days more and I shall gather strength,
Then I am going home."   And home he went,
But to another home than Rannoch side.
Then those kind factory people of themselves
Chose certain men, who, at their charges, bore
His body back to this his native glen,
And placed it down within his father's door.

Upon the coffin was a lid of glass,
Placed there by these same kind and careful hands,
That parents, sisters, brothers, might once more
Look on that face ere dust was strewn on it
For ever. Then they gathered—all his kin,
His friends in youth, those strangers from afar,
And bore him from that farm, and laid him down
Here in this sweet and solitary grave.
And over it the same kind strangers reared
That head-stone, with his name and these few words,
That tell how fervently he sought their good,
How his sweet manners, gentle purity,
Won them, and that for their great love to him,
They carried him that long road that he might rest
Amid his kindred's dust—and he rests well.
But none of his own kindred any more
Shall come to sleep beside him. They are all gone
To find new homes and graves in virgin earth
Beyond Missouri River. None the less
Here he sleeps well, as Duncan over there,
Two student-friends, the flower of Rannoch youth,
Each in his early grave, with Tummel stream
Between them, and Schihallion over all.

Their earthly lore they took from us awhile,
But now they learn the heavenly, and have seen
The secret things that we still wait to know.

Published 1872.

R

III [1]

But one more grave, and that completes the tale
Of Student lads from Rannoch.   Twenty years
And more have vanished, since from yonder farm,
The other side the valley, passed two youths,
Clad in grey hodden, from their own sheep spun,
To the ancient College [2] by the Eastern sea.
Reared amid mountain lonelinesses, where,
Save the shy curlew's call, or wild glead's scream,
No living voices come, they had beheld,
Winter by winter, o'er Schihallion climb
The late cold morn, as they went forth to toil,
Beside their father, in his swampy fields,
About the base of Ben-a-choualach,—
Broad Ben-a-choualach, that stands to guard
The north side of the vale over against
Schihallion, its great brother-sentinel.
There, with all Nature's grandeurs round them shed,
And blending with their daily thoughts and toil,
Their boyhood grew; yet from work out of doors
Leisure of nights and stormy days was saved
For learning; and the village teacher lent
His kindly aid, till, ere the elder saw
His eighteenth summer, they were fit to essay

[1] John Macgregor. [2] University of St. Andrews.

The Student life at College. Forth they fared,
Those simple-hearted lads,—a slender stock
Of home provisions, a few well-worn books,
A father's blessing and a mother's prayers,
All their equipment, as they set their face
Toward that new Student world. How hard it is
To climb the hill of Learning, when young souls
Have early felt the chill of poverty,
And stress of numbing toil, through all their powers!
The elder, Ian, was a climber strong,
In body and mind, to breast the steep himself,
And with a ready hand of help to spare
For his less valiant brother. Many a time,
When I had taught them lore of ancient Rome
Till past noon-tide, ere winter afternoons
In darkness closed, Ian would come and be
My teacher in the language of the Gael.
Strange, old-world names of mountains, corries, burns,
On the smooth side of Loch Rannoch, or the rough,
We conned their meaning o'er. And he would tell
Of dim, old battles, where his outlawed clan,
Along the dusky skirts of Rannoch Moor
Had clashed 'gainst wild Macdonalds of Glencoe,
And gallant Stewarts from Appin. Or he told
Of black bloodhounds let loose by Campbell foes,
From corrie and cairn to hunt his clansmen down
Through long Glen Lyon; and the frantic leap

Over the rock-pent chasm and foaming flood,
And the lorn coronach by his widow wailed
O'er fall'n Macgregor of Rojo. None the less,
But more for these brief Celtic interludes,
He plied the midnight hours, till four full years
Of strenuous study, by the longed-for hope,
A good Degree, were crowned ; and by his aid
The younger brother the same goal attained.
A few more years of poor and patient toil,
Within another seat of learning, gave
To each the full rank of Physician. Then
They took—the brothers took—their separate ways.
Early the younger on the world's high road
Fainted,—the battle was too sore for him ;
He sank ere noon of day, and found a grave
Far from his own Schihallion. Strong of frame,
Well proved in Netley wards, the elder sailed
Physician to a regiment Eastward-bound.
There beneath Indian suns plying his art,
Faithful and kindly, he from comrades won
Liking and much regard, and good repute
With those set over him. Step by step he climbed,
Till he attained an office high in trust,
In old Benares. Then the first to feel
The kind glow of his bettered fortunes were
His parents, whom he summoned to lay down
Their toiling days for comfortable ease,

And the cold Rannoch braeside for the warm,
Well-wooded Vale of Tay. A home therein
He had provided them—a sheltered home—
With a green croft behind, and bright out-look
O'er the clear river to the southern noon.
While there they passed the evening of their days
In quiet, month by month he gladdened them
By letters quaintly writ in Gaelic tongue.
English was but the instrument wherewith
He trafficked with the world ; the Gaelic was
The language of his heart, the only key
That could unlock its secrets. When he met
A Gael on Indian ground, he greeted him
In the dear language ; if he answered well,
That was at once a bond of brotherhood.
And when at length he made himself a home,
To the young prattlers round his knee he told
The mountain legends his own childhood loved,
With Gaelic intermingled. 'Then he took
And blew the big pipe, till the echoes rang,
Through old Benares by the Ganges stream,
With the wild pibrochs of the Highland hills.
While all things seemed with him to prosper most,
Strangely and suddenly there fell on him
A deep, fond yearning for his native land,—
Longing intense to be at home once more.
Just then it chanced that, sore by sickness pressed,

The old man, his father, to the Rannoch farm
Had wandered back, and laid him down to die.
This hearing, homeward Ian set his face
In haste, and reached his native roof in time
Only to hear his father's blessing breathed
From lips already cold. A bleak grey noon
Of May 'twas when they bore the old man forth
Across the vale, and laid him in his rest
Beneath Schihallion, among kindred dead.
There, while his son stood by the open grave,
Bareheaded, the chill east wind through and through
Smote him, enfeebled by the Indian clime.
A few weeks more, and by the self-same road
Him, too, the mourners bore across the vale,
To lay him down close by his father's side,
In that old kirk-yard on the hillock green,
Where is the grave of Ewan Cameron.
Strange by what instinct led, they two alike,
Father and son, sought the old home to die!

And so they rest, all that is mortal rests,
Of those three Students, in their native vale;
Two on this side the Rannoch river, one
Beyond it; and above them evermore
Schihallion's shadow lying, and his peak
Kindling aloft in the first light of dawn.

Written 1881.

VARIA

THE BATTLE OF THE ALMA

    ONCE more the peaceful years
      From their long slumber leap,
And British guns and British cheers
Are thundering by the Pontic deep.
    There the mighty of the West,
      On Humanity's behest,
      France's bravest, England's best,
Are marshalling on the far Sarmatian shore.

    Through that chill dawning grey
      No bugle muster sung,
All noiseless to their war array
From the damp earth the warriors sprung.
    Fair the autumn morning shines
      On the red and azure lines,
      Sweeping o'er the long declines
Between Crimean uplands and the main.

    Lo! where that mountain flank
      Down toward ocean runs,
Legions of Russia, rank o'er rank,
Stand ready by their yawning guns.

THE BATTLE OF THE ALMA

    Yonder France to battle springs,
    Cloud on cloud, her Zouaves flings
    Up the crags, as borne on wings ;
While great broadsides are bellowing on the shore.

    Full on our British front
    The loud hill cannonades,
As full against that awful brunt
Yon Chieftain cheers his brave Brigades.
    Forward, gallant Fusileers !
    Forward, where your Chief appears,
    Young in heart, though blanched with years ;
Who would not follow where he leads the way ?

    Breast-deep the stream they ford,
    The thundering hill-side scale,
While down their close ranks, like a sword,
Shears the broad sheet of iron hail.
    Though the foremost files are low,
    Clutch the colours, upward go,
    Breast to breast against the foe,
And silence those death-breathing guns.

    They are silenced—Fusileers !
    Stern work ye had to do,
Mowed down in front of all your peers,
To Duty and your Country true :

Still from yonder mountain-crown
Dark the battle-front doth frown,
Massive squares are moving down
The current of the conflict back to roll.

Ho! Guardsmen, with your bold
Battalions to the van!
Charge, Clans of Scotland! as of old,
With level bayonets, man to man.
There the Guards, black-helmed and tall
Solid as a rock-hewn wall,
'Gainst the storm of shell and ball
In firm battalions up the mountain move.

And there the Mountaineers,
How terribly they come!
With bayonets down and ringing cheers
Campbells and Camerons charging home.
O to have heard their Highland shout!
Bursting past the dread Redoubt,
When the foemen rolled in rout,
Shrank from the onset of the plaided Clans.

Thou, Leader Chief of all!
Who, battle-days long gone,
Hast stood, while thousands round did fall,
By the right hand of Wellington,

Say, for thou canst witness yield,
Hast thou looked on siege or field,
E'er by braver life-blood sealed,
Than that which consecrateth Alma's hills?

Aye! Britain's standard waves
O'er Alma's uplands bare,
But all its path lies strewn with graves
Of them who died to plant it there!
Gently warrior hands have spread
Green turf o'er their brothers' head;
Leave them there, our noble dead,
Their dust to that far land,—their souls to God.

Written 1854.

GRASMERE

Since our long summer in yon blissful nook,
    Six years, not changeless, intervene ;
Those friends all scattered, I return and look
    Down on this peace serene.

O happy vision ! depth of spirit-balm !
    For hearts that have too deeply yearned,
This still lake holding his majestic calm
    'Mid his green hills inurned.

There dwell, repeated the clear depths among,
    Hills more aerial, skies of fairier cloud,
Hard by, yon homestead, where the summer long
    Our laughters once were loud.

Still gleam the birch-trees down that pass as fair,
    Nor less melodious breaks
The Rotha murmuring down his rocky lair,
    Between his sister lakes.

With the six following poems, published in 1864.

PARTING

O DOOMED to go to sunnier climes,
   With the wa'-gang o' the swallow,
Thee prayers, far-borne from happier times
   And earnest friendship, follow.

Thou leav'st us, ere from moorlands wild
   The plover-flocks have flown,
For lands that have their winters mild,
   As summer in thine own.

Sadly we watch that vessel's track
   O'er the wan autumnal sea,
For spring that brings the swallow back
   Will bring no word of thee.

Thy "wound is deep," earth's balmiest breeze
   Can breathe no healing now:
Those eyes must close on lands and seas,
   To ope, ah! where, and how?

O breathe on him, thou better breath !
  That can the soul-sick heal,
And as the mortal languisheth,
  The immortal life reveal.

POETIC TRUTH

O FOR truth-breathèd music ! soul-like lays !
Not of vain-glory born, nor love of praise,
But welling purely from profound heart-springs,
That lie deep down amid the life of things,
And singing on, heedless though mortal ear
Should never their lone murmur overhear.

When through the world shall voice of poet shine,
Alike true to the human and divine ?
Full of the heart of man, yet fuller fed
At the o'erflow of that divine well-head,
From which, as tiny drops, to earth is brought
Whate'er is pure of love, and true in thought,
To which all spirits, in the flesh that be,
Are as scant rillets to the infinite sea.

PRAYER

Ye tell us prayer is vain—that the divine plan
Disowns it, and as waves in-driven from mid-seas
Break on the headlands, Nature's strong decrees
Dash back his weakness on the heart of man.
Against the universe who can prevail?
Will a voice cleave the everlasting bars?
The heart's poor sigh o'er-soar the loftiest stars
And through all laws to a Divine Will scale?
Too oft will the perplexed soul question thus,
And yet these great laws that encompass us
Of the meanest things on earth consult the weal,
Are very pitiful to the worms and weeds.
Turn they a deaf ear when the warm heart pleads?
He who did plant that heart, will He not feel?

RELIEF

WHO seeketh finds: what shall be his relief
Who hath no power to seek, no heart to pray,
No sense of God, but bears as best he may,
A lonely incommunicable grief?
What shall he do? One only thing he knows,
That his life flits a frail uneasy spark
In the great vast of universal dark,
And that the grave may not be all repose.
Be still, sad soul! lift thou no passionate cry,
But spread the desert of thy being bare
To the full searching of the All-seeing eye:
Wait—and through dark misgiving, blank despair,
God will come down in pity, and fill the dry
Dead place with light, and life, and vernal air.

MEMORIES

As the far seen peaks of Alpine ranges
   In their robe of virgin snow endure,
High o'er Europe plains and earthborn changes,
   Calmly and imperishably pure;

Thus, e'en thus, so lofty and so holy,
   O'er our poor life's ordinary moods
High aloof, yet very loving and lowly,
   Shine the blessèd Christ's Beatitudes.

Near them Paul's pure charity eternal
   Dwelling keeps, above earth's cloudy clime,
Beckoning worn hearts upward by its vernal
   Brightness from these murky flats of time.

And from off those summits do not voices,
   All divine, yet very human, come?
Hearing which awe-struck the soul rejoices,
   As at echoes from a long-lost home.

Deem not these are young earth's hymeneal
　　Chaunts, no after age can e'er repeat;
Something all at variance with the real
　　World that meets us in the field and street.

Doth not memory from the past recover
　　Some who near us once did move and breathe,
Names, that as we read those high words over,
　　Fitly might be written underneath?

Blessèd gifts of God, that our poor weakness
　　Might not only hear, but soothly see,
What of truth and love, what might of meekness,
　　In our flesh in very deed might be.

While they here sojourned their presence drew us
　　By the sweetness of their human love,
Day by day good thoughts of them renew us,
　　Like fresh tidings from the world above;

Coming, like the stars at gloamin' glinting
　　Through the western clouds, when loud winds cease,
Silently of that calm country hinting,
　　Where they with the angels are at peace.

Not their own, ah! not from earth was flowing
　　That high strain to which their souls were tuned,

Year by year we saw them inly growing
   Liker Him with Whom their hearts communed.

Then to Him they passed ; but still unbroken,
   Age to age, lasts on that goodly line,
Whose pure lives are, more than all words spoken,
   Earth's best witness to the life divine.

Subtlest thought shall fail, and learning falter,
   Churches change, forms perish, systems go,
But our human needs, they will not alter,
   Christ no after age shall e'er outgrow.

Yea, amen ! O changeless One, Thou only
   Art life's guide and spiritual goal,
Thou the Light across the dark vale lonely,—
   Thou the eternal haven of the soul !

HIDDEN LIFE

Ay, true it is, our dearest, best beloved,
   Of us unknowing, are by us unknown,
That from our outward survey far removed,
   Deep down they dwell, unfathomed and alone.

We gaze on their loved faces, hear their speech,
   The heart's most earnest utterance,—yet we feel
Something beyond, nor they nor we can reach,
   Something they never can on earth reveal.

Dearly they loved us, we returned our best,
   They passed from earth, and we divined them not,
As though the centre of each human breast
   Were a sealed chamber of unuttered thought.

Hidden from others do we know ourselves?
   Albeit the surface takes the common light;
Who hath not felt that this our being shelves
   Down to abysses, dark and infinite?

HIDDEN LIFE

As to the sunlight some basaltic isle
   Upheaves a scanty plain, far out from shore,
But downward plungeth sheer walls many a mile,
   'Neath the unsunned ocean floor.

So some small light of consciousness doth play
   On the surface of our being, but the broad
And permanent foundations every way
   Pass into mystery, are hid in God.

The last outgoings of our wills are ours;
   What moulded them, and fashioned down below,
And gave the bias to our nascent powers,
   We cannot grasp nor know.

O Thou on Whom our blind foundations lean,
   In Whose hand our wills' primal fountains be,
We cannot—but Thou canst—O make them clean!
   We cast ourselves on Thee.

From the foundations of our being breathe
   Up all their darkened pores pure light of Thine,
Till, in that light transfigured from beneath,
   We in Thy countenance shine.

I HAVE a life with CHRIST to live,
But, ere I live it, must I wait
Till learning can clear answer give
   Of this and that book's date?

I have a life in CHRIST to live,
I have a death in CHRIST to die;—
And must I wait, till science give
   All doubts a full reply?

Nay rather, while the sea of doubt
Is raging wildly round about,
Questioning of life and death and sin,
   Let me but creep within
Thy fold, O CHRIST, and at Thy feet
   Take but the lowest seat,
And hear Thine awful voice repeat
In gentlest accents, heavenly sweet,
   Come unto Me, and rest:
   Believe Me, and be blest.

Written 1868.

'Twixt gleams of joy and clouds of doubt
  Our feelings come and go;
Our best estate is tossed about
  In ceaseless ebb and flow.

No mood of feeling, form of thought,
  Is constant for a day;
But Thou, O Lord! Thou changest not;
  The same Thou art alway.

I grasp Thy strength, make it mine own,
  My heart with peace is blest;
I lose my hold, and then comes down
  Darkness and cold unrest.

Let me no more my comfort draw
  From my frail hold of Thee,—
In this alone rejoice with awe;
  Thy mighty grasp of me.

Out of that weak unquiet drift
    That comes but to depart,
To that pure Heaven my spirit lift
    Where Thou unchanging art.

Lay hold of me with Thy strong grasp,
    Let Thy Almighty arm
In its embrace my weakness clasp,
    And I shall fear no harm.

Thy purpose of eternal good
    Let me but surely know;
On this I'll lean, let changing mood
    And feeling come or go;

Glad when Thy sunshine fills my soul;
    Not lorn when clouds o'ercast;
Since Thou within Thy sure control
    Of love dost hold me fast.

Written 1871.

ILLUSTRATIVE NOTES

ILLUSTRATIVE NOTES

Page 3. *Glen Desseray* appeared in *The Celtic Magazine*, 1877, preceded by the note subjoined :—

"The following poem attempts to reproduce facts heard, and impressions received, during the wanderings of several successive summers among the scenes which are here described. Whatever view political economists may take of these events, it can hardly be denied that the form of human society, and the phase of human suffering, here attempted to be described, deserve at least some record. If the lesser incidents of the poem are not all literally exact, of the main outlines and leading events of the simple story it may well be said, 'It's an ower true tale.'

"The story is supposed to be told by a grandson of the Ewen Cameron, and a nephew of the Angus Cameron of the poem—one who, as a boy, had seen and shared in the removal of the people from his native glen."

The scene is laid in the two great glens which open towards Loch Arkaig on the north.

This Poem is printed from a Text which had the Author's own corrections attached to it, and a few omissions have now been made, for the purpose of carrying out wishes more than once expressed by him.

Page 13. *Shinty fray.*—A game in which bats, somewhat resembling golf-clubs, are used. There are two goals called "hails"; the object of each party being to drive the ball beyond their opponent's *hail.—Jamieson.*

Page 15. *Loop.*—The English word "loop" is used as, perhaps, the best to represent the far more expressive Gaelic word *luib*, which is applied to windings or bends of rivers.— J. C. S.

Page 35.
*Never while I breathe shall mortal
Grasp this hand which touched the Prince:—*

This is literally true of Hugh Chisholm, one of the seven men who sheltered the Prince, on his way north, in the Cave of Corombian. Chisholm went afterwards to reside in Edinburgh, where many called on him out of curiosity, to see one who had been such a devoted adherent of Prince Charlie. Chisholm received money from several of these admirers, and in return, while thanking them, he always offered them a shake of his left hand, excusing himself for not giving the right, by saying that since he had shaken hands with the bonnie Prince at parting, he resolved never to give his right hand to any man, until he saw the Prince again.

Page 60. *Has-wool.*—See Burns's song, "I coft a stane o' haslock woo'." "Haslock, or hauselock wool is the softest and finest of the fleece, and is shorn from the throats of sheep in summer heat, to give them air and keep them cool."—*Allan Cunningham:*—J. C. S.

Page 88. *The Mountain Walk.* — In his "Mountain Walk" Shairp was accompanied by an intelligent old Highlander from Kilmallie, whose forefathers had resided for many generations among the glens at the head of Loch Arkaig. The country which they traversed forms the western portion of the mainland of Inverness-shire. It is of vast extent, and from the inaccessibleness of its situation, the wildness of its scenery, and the sparseness of its population, it is emphatically denominated throughout the Highlands as, Na Garbh-chriochan—*i.e. The* Rough Bounds. Among the corries and caves of this remote region, Prince Charles Edward and some of his most distinguished followers sought conceal-ment after Culloden. In the wanderings of the young Prince, Shairp was deeply interested. Throughout his life he retained a very vivid recollection of the scenery described in this poem.

Writing a few years ago to an old St. Andrews student, who resided near Loch Arkaig, he made minute inquiries as to the route the Prince had taken when on a certain occasion he was closely surrounded by troops. In the course of his letter he described the scene, giving the local names, and expressing an opinion as to a particular "pass" through which he supposed the escape to have been effected.

This poem should be read in connection with *Glen Desseray*.

Page 98. *Glen-Sallach*.—Near Kildalloig in Argyle, the home of the author's mother. He was taken there as a young child, and the impression left on him by the glen was never effaced.

Page 106. *Sli'-Gaoil*.—The legend is of the death of Diarmid, founder of the Clan Campbell. He slew, at Torintuirc, West Loch Tarbert, Argyleshire, a poisonous boar that had long infested the district, and while measuring it had one of his hands pierced with a bristle. As he was bleeding to death from the wound, he wished to be taken to where he could see the Sliabh (Sleeav), and looking towards it he said :—

> Sliabh mo gaol, sliabh mo gaol s' mo chaisd,
> Cha deide misse suas go brach,
> S' cha chairren usa anuas am' feist.

that is,

> Mountain of my love, mountain of my love, and my darling,
> I will not go up—for ever,
> And thou wilt not come down—ever.

Sli' (*i.e.* Sliabh) Gaoil is a lofty mountain near Kilberry.

Page 110. *Cailleach Bein-y-Vreich* (Beinn-a'-Bhric).—The Cailleach was a beanshith or fairy that often appeared to hunters in the gloaming of summer evenings, gathering and milking the hinds on a hillside, while she sang some wild air, such as dairy-maids still use to soothe the cow while she is being milked. She was very tall, and wore on her head a spotted kerchief, and her long grey locks waved over her shoulders. Sometimes she wore hose, but often she was seen with no covering below the ankle.

She always wore a yellow robe about her. In winter she was often seen *by women*, driving her herd of deer to the shore; and they said that when she took the form of a grey deer, their kailyards suffered. She denies this in her song, however. If any hunter saw the Cailleach, he knew well it was useless for him to roam the forest that day. One time, in spite of her having been seen, a Lochaber hunter went to the hill in search of deer. When he had spent the whole day in wandering, without coming upon any deer, and he was engaged lighting a fire, and singing the verses accompanying an air which he composed as he went on, suddenly, when he looked up, after the fifth verse was completed, he saw the Cailleach, who continued the song from the fifth verse to the end.—*Seul Gorm* (p. 111) appears to be a poetic name: *Seul*, gem: *Gorm*, blue—The Blue Jewel.

Page 121. *The wild kerne.*—Irish troops in the army of Edward I in the campaign of 1298. *Sir Neil.*—The places here referred to are to be found in the Pass of Brander, near Oban. This was the scene of many sanguinary conflicts.—See Introduction and Notes to Scott's *Highland Widow.*:

The following is from *The Statistical Account of Scotland:*—"MacPhaidan, an Irishman, who was serviceable to Edward I when engaged in his attempt to subvert the independence of Scotland, and to whom that monarch, in 1297, made a grant for his services of the lordship of Argyle and Lorn, was attacked by Sir William Wallace, and defeated A.D. 1300, at the north-east side of Ben Cruachan, near to the Pass of Brainder. Wallace on his way to Argyleshire was met in Glendochart by Sir Neil Campbell, knight of Lochaw, with 300 men. They found MacPhaidan posted at Ben Cruachan. The onset is said to have been keen. Many hundreds of MacPhaidan's followers were driven to the lake and drowned; and though he himself, with fifteen men, fled to a neighbouring cave in the face of Craig-an-Araidh, his retreat was discovered and he was there slain."

Sir Neil Campbell was an ancestor of J. C. Shairp through the Campbells of Auchinbreck.

Page 124. *Duncan Bàn MacIntyre.*—An excellent sketch of his life and account of his poetry, with specimens translated by Shairp, will be found in his *Aspects of Poetry*, chap. x: Oxford, 1881.

Page 130. *Glen Torridon.*—It is situated in the north-west of Ross-shire, in the peninsula between Loch Carron and Loch Torridon.

Page 134. *Loch Torridon.*—This poem and *Loch Ericht*, p. 159, appear never to have received the writer's final touches.

Page 162. *October.*—The neighbourhood of Cuil-a-luinn, Aberfeldy, on the Tay, Shairp's Highland home in summer and autumn, is described in this playful imitation of the delightful English Autumn scene by Keats.

Page 164. *Garth Castle.*—Alexander Stuart, son of King Robert II., commonly known, for his ferocity, as the Wolf of Badenoch, burnt the cathedral and town of Elgin, owing to a quarrel with the bishop. He is said to have built Garth Castle, and to have founded the family of the Stuarts of Garth, who possessed it till recent times. His tomb, surmounted by a marble effigy, is still to be seen in the cathedral of Dunkeld.—J. C. S.

Page 172. *Drumuachdar.*—This ballad from the Badenoch country is given as a specimen of Shairp's translations from the Gaelic. The incident upon which the elegy is founded, according to a writer in *The Celtic Magazine* for May 1887, (who gives the original words), must have occurred in the last century. "The cattle, at Blargie, in Upper Badenoch, being let loose on a sunny day in early spring, became frantic with delight of their novel and unexpectedly-acquired freedom, and betook themselves to the hills, heedless of consequences. The herd—a young man named Macdonald—followed them as far as Drumuachdar, which extends between Dalwhinnie and Dalnacardoch. While he traversed that solitary and sterile tract, the weather, then proverbially fickle, changed terribly. A blinding snowstorm set in; and the unfortunate lad never more found his way home." The elegy is said to have been poured forth by Macdonald's True-love, who joined in the search for him.

The Rev. T. Sinton of Glengarry states that the copy of the Gaelic original with which he supplied Shairp was fragmentary.

Page 174. *Kiln.*—Mr. Sinton writes:—"A kiln for hardening corn preparatory to grinding was to be found in connection with every *town*. The actual kiln was situated at one end of a house to which it gave its name. It was in this building that the body of the dead herd was laid—much to the grief of his friends. For the kiln was reckoned a place of evil omen. Generally it was the scene of all the *uncanny* events of the *town*. Therefore it was that when Cluny—the leading man of the country—arrived, he immediately ordered Macdonald's body to be removed from the kiln.

Until quite recently Highland gentlemen attended the humblest funerals in their neighbourhood; and the people always expected their presence at the scene of any untoward event such as that which forms the theme of this ballad."

Page 182. *Thrieve Castle.*—This is the ancient seat of the Douglases, in Kirkcudbright, on an island in the Dee. William, eighth Earl of Douglas, who defied James II, imprisoned in Thrieve Castle, in 1452, Maclellan, guardian of Lord Bombie, the ancestor of the Earls of Kirkcudbright. When James sent Sir Patrick Gray with a letter requesting the release of the prisoner, William insisted on his visiter dining before business, and meanwhile had Maclellan beheaded in the castle court. After dinner he read the King's letter, and then, in professed deference to his injunctions, offered Gray the body, saying that he had possessed himself of the head some time before. This haughty act led to Douglas's own death soon afterwards.

Page 185. *Devorguilla.*—New, or Sweetheart Abbey, is pleasantly situated eight miles south of Dumfries. It was erected in 1275 by Devorguilla, in memory of her husband, John Baliol. She had had his heart embalmed and placed in an ornamented ivory case; and when she died this was laid on her bosom, and buried with her, in accordance with her own instructions. Thus originated the romantic name of the Abbey.

Page 201. *Three Friends in Yarrow.*—Edmund Lushington, some time Professor of Greek in Glasgow,—Professor

Veitch,—and the Author.—*Piers Cockburn;* see "Lament of the Border Widow," in *The Minstrelsy of the Scottish Border.* The Editor has put *than* for *as* in stanza 15 : but Shairp uses *as* for *than* elsewhere.

Page 203. *The Flower of Yarrow Vale.*—The reference is to Mary Scott, daughter of John Scott of Dryhope. She was called "The Flower of Yarrow," and was married in 1576 to Walter Scott of Harden, afterwards known as "Auld Wat," a famous man on the Borders. According to the tradition, Dryhope was to keep Harden in man's meat and horse's meat for a year and a day, and, after the marriage, five barons engaged that Harden should remove from Dryhope Tower at the expiry of the stipulated period. Harden, on his part, was to give Dryhope the fruits of the first raid under the Michaelmas moon. Under the marriage contract Harden endows his bride with certain of his lands, and Dryhope engages to give his daughter 400 merks Scots, "at the time of the said Walter and Marion's passing to their 'awin hous.'"—The Author of the poem was a lineal descendant of Mary Scott of Dryhope.

Page 228. *Spring,* 1876 : Stanza 6.—Mr. T. Bayne writes : "Henry Alexander Douglas, brother-in-law of Principal Shairp, had been one of his earliest friends at Glasgow University. He was a distinguished English churchman, and became Bishop of Bombay. He died in 1875, and his burial-place is under Weem Craig, near the River Tay."

Stanza 7.—These lines refer to Dr. Norman Macleod (Barony Church, Glasgow), one of the most widely-known Scotsmen of the nineteenth century.

The lifelong friendship between Macleod and Shairp began in 1837, at Glasgow University, where they constantly met, reading often together, with intense enjoyment, Wordsworth's Poems, and having many common sympathies. Dr. Macleod's grave is at Campsie, in Stirlingshire, his early home. "On the one side are the hum of business and the houses of toiling humanity. On the other green pastoral hills and the silence of Highland solitudes." See *Memoirs of Dr. Norman Macleod,* by his brother, Incumbent of Park Church, Glasgow.

Page 231. *Highland Students.*—Duncan Campbell, M.A., St. Andrews : died at Bridgend, Rannoch, 11th June 1867, aged 23 years. Rev. Ewan Cameron, Pastor of Baptist Church, Quarmby Oaks, Yorkshire : died 6th July 1867. John Macgregor entered the Bengal Medical Service : died at Drumglass, Rannoch, 22d June 1881, aged 39 years.

All were students at St. Andrews whilst J. C. Shairp held the post of Professor of Humanity.

INDEX OF FIRST LINES

	PAGE
A bowshot from the loch aloof	159
Again the bonny blue bells	191
As the far seen peaks of Alpine ranges	259
A time there was	188
Ay, true it is, our dearest, best-beloved	262
Beyond the bay, beyond the gleaming sands	231
By the wee birchen corries lie patches of green	112
Child of the far-off ocean flood	134
Darling Flowers! at last I've found you	153
Days on days, the East wind blowing	167
Doth Yarrow flow endeared by dream	195
Down to Loch Nevish went the day	36
Early young Angus rose to meet	45
Eighty years have come and gone	3
From beaten paths and common tasks reprieved	88
Garth Castle, he hath borne the brunt	164
Guest! but no stranger,—many a time before	221
Ha! there he comes, the headlong Highland River	144
Hath then that life-long combatant with death	225

	PAGE
I have a life with CHRIST to live	264
In grey Criffel's lap of granite	185
In this bare treeless forest lone	106
I watched the sun fall down with prone descent	128
Land of bens and glens and corries	114
No softer south than this did ever fall	228
October misty bright, the touch is thine	162
O doomed to go to sunnier climes	254
O'er the dreary moor of Rannoch	100
O for truth-breathèd music ! soul-like lays	256
O how my heart lap to her	193
Oh wherefore cam ye here, Ailie	146
O many a year is gone, since in life's fresh dawn	201
O marvellous Glen of Torridon	130
O mountain stream ! so old, yet ever young	170
Once more by mighty Cruachan, and once more	119
Once more the peaceful years	249
On the braes around Glenfinnan	108
O the Border Hills sae green	198
O wae on Loch Laggan !	172
Seven Summers long had fired the glens	68
Since our long summer in yon blissful nook	253
Soon as the kindling dawn had tipt	53
Still let me dive the glens among	157
That summer glen is far away	98
The homes long are gone, but enchantment still lingers	124
The showers are over, the skiffing showers	149
The spray may drive, the rain may pour	104
These hoary, dialed, belfry Towers	223
'Twixt gleams of joy and clouds of doubt	265

INDEX OF FIRST LINES

PAGE

Up the long corrie, through the screetan rents	140
Weird wife of Bein-y-Vreich ! horo ! horo	110
Whence should ye o'er gentle spirits	182
When early morning o'er the mountains high	139
When from copse, and craig, and summit	22
Who seeketh finds : what shall be his relief	258
Will ye gang wi' me and fare	179
Within the ancient College-gate I passed	209
Ye tell us prayer is vain—that the divine plan	257

THE END

Printed by R. & R. CLARK, *Edinburgh.*

www.ingramcontent.com/pod-product-compliance
Lightning Source LLC
Chambersburg PA
CBHW022102230426
43672CB00008B/1260